The State Rehabilitation Council-

Vocational Rehabilitation Partnership

Under WIOA

Please use the following citation when referencing, reproducing, or utilizing information obtained from this resource.

McGuire-Kuletz, M., Tomlinson, P., & Hurley, K.B. (2019). *The State Rehabilitation Council–vocational rehabilitation partnership under WIOA*–Washington, DC: The George Washington University, Center for Rehabilitation Counseling Research and Education.

The original contents of this document, published in 2010, were developed under a grant (H264C090004) from the U.S. Department of Education's Rehabilitation Services Administration awarded to The George Washington University. The contents of this revised document, nor the original contents, necessarily represent the policy of those agencies, and endorsement by the federal government or the university should not be assumed.

The current edition reflects changes in legislation and policy subsequent to the original publication (2010), and has not been vetted or endorsed by the U.S. Department of Education or The George Washington University.

Table of Contents

Page

Rewrite Team vi

Preface 1
The Consumer Voice 1
How to Use This Publication 2

Chapter 1: History and Law 3
Legislative History of Vocational Rehabilitation 3
The 1992 Amendments and SRCs..4
The 1998 Amendments and SRCs..5
Title I (VR Services) Principles...8
The 2014 Amendments and SRCs..8
SRC Composition and Functions as Outlined in Section 105..............................9
Other SRC Mandates in Title I 13
Legislative Process...14
Conclusion 15
References...15

Chapter 2: SRC Basics 16
Composition...16
Legal Basis for SRCs..17
Organizational Variation 17
Appointment and Terms of Service...18
Continuous Recruitment 19
Orientation 21
Ongoing Training...22
Role of the Chair and Vice Chair 23
Committees 24
Summary and Recommendations 26
References..26

Chapter 3: SRC Business Practices...27
Developing a Mission Statement 27
Scheduling Meetings 28
Facilitating Effective Meetings and Council Communication 29
Establishing Committee Structure and Duties 29
Retaining Active Members 31
Developing Bylaws 32
Developing a Resource Plan 34
Summary 36
References 36

Chapter 4: Implementation of Responsibilities..37
Performance Evaluation: "Review, Analyze and Advise"..37
Common Performance Measures..38
Budget and Expenditure Information 39
Policy Information..40
Management Information 41
Order of Selection...41
Unified or Combined State Plan 43
Comprehensive System of Personnel Development...43
Partnerships...44
The SRC Role in the Comprehensive Statewide Needs Assessment 44
Participation of the SRC with the State Agency in the Monitoring 45
Consumer Satisfaction Survey...46
Public Participation...47
Selection and Evaluation of Impartial Hearing Officers 48
Advocacy 48
Summary..49
References...49

Chapter 5: SRC Resources 50
Rehabilitation Act of 1973, as Amended...50
Rehabilitation Services Administration...50
VR Federal Regulations...51
State VR Agency Websites...51
National Coalition of State Rehabilitation Councils 51
Client Assistance Program..51
Parent Training and Information Centers 52
Statewide Independent Living Council and Centers for Independent Living 52
Communication Tools 52
Council of State Administrators of Vocational Rehabilitation...................................52
National Council of State Agencies for the Blind 53
Consortia of Administrators for Native American Rehabilitation.................................53
National Clearinghouse for Rehabilitation Training Materials 54
Resources for Consumer Satisfaction Surveys 54
National Rehabilitation Association 54
Councils on Developmental Disabilities 54
Institute on Rehabilitation Issues..55
Disability.gov...55
U.S. Census Bureau: American FactFinder..55
Disability and Business Technical Assistance Center 55
U.S. Government Accountability Office 55
Ticket to Work...56
Assistive Technology Act Programs 56
O*NET..56
Job Accommodations Network...56
Office of Employment and Disability Policy 57

Protection and Advocacy Systems...57
National Institute on Disability and Rehabilitation Research..57
VR Needs Assessment Guide 57
RSA Monitoring and Technical Assistance Guide 57
Annual Disability Statistics Compendium...58
Conclusion 58

Appendix A: Major RSA Policy Guidance Documents Related to the VR Program............**59**

Appendix B: Frequently Used Acronyms--**60**

Appendix C: Code of Federal Regulations, Title 34, Part 361- State Vocational Rehabilitatiom Services Program.. **64**

Appendix D: Introduction to Robert's Rules of Order...**78**

Appendix E: What Are Other SRCs Doing? Where Can I Find Examples?..................**81**
Section 1: Example of SRC Bylaws...82
Section 2: Example of SRC Handbook...87
Section 3: Example of SRC Operating Procedures...96
Section 4: Example of SRC Input to the Unified State Plan...101
Section 5: Example of SRC Guidebook for RSA Monitoring Visit..................................108
Section 6: Example Worksheet: Membership Composition Mandate................................109

Rewrite Team

Maureen McGuire-Kuletz
Center for Rehabilitation Counseling Research
& Education
413 John Carlyle Street
2nd Floor – Room 233
Alexandria, VA 22314
Phone: 202-994-9428
mkuletz@gwu.edu

Joan Holleran
Retired, New Hampshire Vocational
Rehabilitation
119 Main Street, Unit 1
New London, NH 03257
jeholleran@tds.net

Katherine B. Hurley
Center for Rehabilitation Counseling Research
& Education
413 John Carlyle Street
2nd Floor – Room 233
Alexandria, VA 22314
Phone: 202-994-1511
Email: kbhurley@gwu.edu

Thomas G. Jennings
Retired NJ Vocational Rehabilitation
New Jersey SRC
4 Cook Street
Monmouth Beach, NJ 07750
Phone: 732-233-4583
tomjennings07@verizon.net

Deborah L. Lovely
Retired WV Vocational Rehabilitation
905 Geary Road
South Charleston, WV 25303
(304) 744-6074
d_lovely@hotmail.com

Graham Sisson, Jr.
SRC General Counsel/Liaison
560 S. Lawrence Street
Montgomery, AL 36104
Phone: 334-293-7189
Graham.sisson@rehab.alabama.gov

Sherry Taylor
West Virginia State Rehabilitation Council
Executive Director
Vice President & Treasurer of National
Coalition of SRCs
107 Capitol Street
Charleston, WV 25301
Phone: 304-356-2089 office
Cell: 304-561-4846
sherry.a.taylor@wv.gov

Pat Tomlinson
Retired NJ Vocational Rehabilitation
New Jersey SRC
268 Bayshore Drive
Brick, NJ 08723
Phone: 732-539-4306
mandalay@comcast.net

Linda Vegoe
Retired Wisconsin Client Assistance Program
Director and SRC Chairperson
7426 Country Club Rd.
Oshkosh, WI 54902
920-419-0807
pack4vr@ntd.net

Pisnu Bua-lam
Deputy Director WV Division of
Rehabilitation Services
107 Capitol Street
Charleston, WV 25301
Phone: 304-356-2088
pisnu.bua-iam@wv.gov

Special thanks to West Virginia staff Joseph (Zeke) Hampton and Doug Snuffer who assisted with Chapter 4.

Preface

This document is intended to facilitate strong partnerships between State Rehabilitation Councils (SRCs) and state vocational rehabilitation (VR) agencies consistent with the principles articulated in Section 100(a) of the Rehabilitation Act of 1973 (the Act). This publication provides guidance and support to states as they partner in a mutually beneficial manner on behalf of people with disabilities. The partnership described in the Act is unique and calls upon SRCs and VR to jointly conduct business with the primary focus of successful employment outcomes for people with disabilities. The wonderful challenge is to blend the sharing of responsibility with the talent of the partners who come to the table.

Fortunately for individuals with disabilities in the United States, crafters of the Act, as amended, identified a significant need for SRCs and VR to contribute equally in the accomplishment of certain tasks. The intent of the partnership—to share responsibility for the development of specific products and outcomes while advocating on behalf of individuals with disabilities—is critical to ensure full inclusion in employment and integration into society for people with disabilities.

The SRC-VR partnership includes several key required activities and demands a spirit of respect and collaboration. These activities have a major impact on the ability of VR to accomplish its primary objectives as outlined in the law. The SRC-VR partnership is only as strong as the relationship that exists between the SRC chair and VR director, who set the tone for the full membership and staff.

The Consumer Voice

SRCs are the consumer voice for the VR program. Federally mandated membership requirements include a broad range of stakeholders to ensure that various constituencies have a voice in the conduct of the VR agency. This consumer voice is absolutely necessary for the VR program to partner with individuals with disabilities to *jointly* facilitate the accomplishment of their dreams of independence, full community integration, and employment.

SRC members represent the state agency to a broad array of partners such as employers, parents, educators, community rehabilitation programs, and other stakeholders in the VR program. They reinforce the value that individuals with disabilities are able to achieve quality employment outcomes and become contributing members of society.

Though mandated by federal law, the partnership between SRCs and VR extends beyond the shared accomplishment of mandated tasks. Specifically, the partnership is a call to action to advocate for and to hear the voices of the people served by VR. The partnership must be a commitment and priority for the partners in order to make the VR system a change agent whose goal is to assist people with disabilities to become employed in integrated, competitive employment!

The authors of this publication hope that you will find information and tools to help your state develop and maintain strong partnerships between the SRC and VR to fully implement the spirit of the law. As you read, we are sure you will find that the SRC-VR partnership demonstrates that working together works!

How to Use This Publication

The organization of this publication is intended to provide maximum flexibility to the reader. The text is designed for SRC members, VR staff, and other stakeholders such as individuals with disabilities and community rehabilitation providers. Though the full monograph may be used in its entirety for training purposes, each chapter is crafted to be used independently of the rest of the document as needed. Additionally, several appendices include examples of SRC bylaws, handbooks, and major VR program policy guidance.

Acronyms are spelled out at first use in each chapter. They can also be accessed alphabetically in Appendix B.

Chapter 1:
History and Law

Legislative History of Vocational Rehabilitation

In discussing the importance of State Rehabilitation Councils (SRCs), how they evolved, and their relationship to the public vocational rehabilitation (VR) program, it is important to review the legislative history that created and expanded the SRC's role to its current form. A review of the major legislation that improved the public VR program clearly reveals Congress's intent over the years to more meaningfully involve individuals with disabilities and the rehabilitation community in partnership with VR.

The following listing illustrates the legislative progression of the public VR program:

- **1918:** The Soldier's Rehabilitation Act was established for rehabilitation of returning veterans.
- **1920:** The Smith-Fess Act was created to provide a program of rehabilitation for citizens with disabilities. It was strengthened by the success of the Soldier's Rehabilitation Act of 1918.
- **1930:** Public Law 317 extended the civilian VR act for an additional 3 years. It required states to match federal funds.
- **1935:** The state-federal program of VR was strengthened and extended. Congress was now authorized to support VR as a continuous program. The National Rehabilitation Association played a major role in this legislation.
- **1936:** The Randolph-Sheppard Act was authorized and required states to license qualified personnel who are blind to operate vending stands in federal buildings or federally sponsored buildings.
- **1938:** The Javits-Wagner-O'Day Act was passed, requiring all federal agencies to purchase specified supplies and services from nonprofit agencies employing persons who are blind or have other significant disabilities. It was amended in 1971 to become the AbilityOne Program.
- **1943:** In Public Law 113, the 78th Congress authorized major amendments to broaden the VR program. For the first time, medical, surgical, and other physical restoration services were authorized, and persons with mental health conditions and cognitive or other intellectual disabilities were eligible to apply for services. The amendments allowed states to split rehabilitation for the blind from general agencies and establish separate blind agencies.
- **1954:** The Vocational Rehabilitation Act Amendments of 1954, Public Law 565, typified the people-oriented character of the rehabilitation movement. The provisions of the new law were clearly intended to bring the public and voluntary agencies into a closer working alliance.
- **1965:** Extended evaluation was introduced to determine eligibility. The National Commission on Architectural Barriers to Rehabilitation of the Handicapped was established.

- **1973:** The Rehabilitation Act was comprehensively rewritten, with priority placed on services for individuals with severe disabilities. The individualized written rehabilitation program was created, which was intended to make the client a full partner in the rehabilitation process. Title V, the protection for certain civil rights for people with disabilities, was established. The Client Assistance Program was established.
- **1978:** The national independent living program was established.
- **1986:** Supported employment and rehabilitation engineering were added as services.
- **1992:** Consumer-controlled Statewide Rehabilitation Advisory Councils and State Independent Living Councils were established. Consumer choice was emphasized. The eligibility requirements were changed, requiring the VR agency to demonstrate that an individual could not benefit from VR services before determining ineligibility. Consumer participation in the individualized written rehabilitation program was strengthened.
- **1998:** The public VR program became Title IV of the Workforce Investment Act. "State Rehabilitation Advisory Councils" were changed to "State Rehabilitation Councils." The informed consumer choice mandate was strengthened. "Individualized written rehabilitation program" was changed to "individualized plan for employment." A mediation option was added to the appeal process. Interagency agreements with higher education were mandated.
- **2014:** The public VR program was reauthorized as Title IV of the Workforce Innovation and Opportunity Act (WIOA)(P.L. 114–95). There were no major changes to SRC duties. WIOA changed "competitive employment" to "competitive integrated employment", required VR to expend at least 15% of its overall federal budget on pre-employment transition services (Pre-ETS), restricted further the payment of subminimum wages under Section 511, and mandated greater partnership among the core workforce system partners.

The 1992 Amendments and SRCs

When the reauthorization of the Rehabilitation Act amendments was being considered by the 102nd Congress in 1992, the call for more involvement by individuals with disabilities in the VR program was intensifying. Because disability rights advocates had begun to find their voice through a new and active role in the fashioning of the 1986 amendments to the Rehabilitation Act, this activism helped to enhance the message that any changes to the 72-year-old statute should be done with individuals with disabilities "at the table."

The concepts of consumer control and empowerment were brought forth in the 1992 amendments in various ways throughout the reauthorization process. As Representative Major Owens (D-NY) stated during that body's final consideration of the Conference Committee's Report on H.R. 5482, "I am pleased that the House and Senate have reached agreement on the issues addressed by this bill. H.R. 5482 creates partnerships between providers and consumers to ensure a more consumer driven system" (Congressional Record, 1992a).

Senator David Durenberger (R-MN), ranking minority member of the Senate Subcommittee on Disability Policy, commented during the Senate debate:

> In this reauthorization, we have done all that was possible to continue to widen the door and expand opportunities for consumers. Some of the major accomplishments include: A revision of the act that ensures the concepts of empowerment for individuals with disabilities will be followed, including respect for individual dignity, self-determination,

inclusion, integration, and full participation of individuals with disabilities; . . . the establishment of a State Rehabilitation Advisory Council for the basic grant program, a majority of whose members shall be persons with disabilities. (Congressional Record, 1992b)

Both the House of Representatives and the Senate included in their respective bills (H.R. 5482 and S. 3065) the requirement that the state VR plan include an assurance that each state VR agency establish a state advisory committee. The House bill referred to the newly created entity as the Rehabilitation Consumer and Business Advisory Council, and the Senate amendment called it the State Rehabilitation Advisory Committee. The Committee of Conference Report accepted the Senate's language.

The 1998 Amendments and SRCs

Consumer empowerment and the SRC's role in partnering with VR were recognized and considerably strengthened in the 1998 amendments, as evidenced by the following excerpts from a Senate committee report.

> The committee recognizes the need for the disability community in a State to play a significant role in ensuring that the vocational rehabilitation program operates effectively. Therefore, the committee, in several respects, significantly strengthens the role of the State Rehabilitation Council (formerly named the State Rehabilitation Advisory Council) in developing policies, planning activities, evaluating program effectiveness, and carrying out other functions related to the vocational rehabilitation program. The committee bill requires that the Council, in conjunction with the State vocational rehabilitation agency, jointly conduct the comprehensive needs assessment of individuals with disabilities in the State, develop (and agree to) the State's annual goals and priorities in carrying out the vocational rehabilitation program, and evaluate the State's performance relative to its goals on an annual basis. Additional sections of the S. 1579, including sections 101(a)(21) and 105 of the Act, build upon the existing Council role by specifying its broad responsibilities to assist the State vocational rehabilitation agency in, for example, developing all portions of the State plan and amendments thereto, as well as policies, procedures, and reports related to the vocational rehabilitation program. Through the bill the committee recognizes that the Council's role in some States is not purely advisory and in other States is evolving to reflect a true partnership between the Council and the State vocational rehabilitation agency in ensuring that individuals with disabilities receive appropriate, timely, and effective vocational rehabilitation services. (Senate Committee on Labor and Human Resources, 1998, p. 17)

The Committee of Conference Report included a grandfathering clause for states that already had a "consumer controlled independent commission." Such states were allowed to retain those structures rather than establish a State Rehabilitation Advisory Council as required by the legislation.

Regarding council membership, the committee
- Added at least one representative from the statewide workforce investment partnership, a representative from a project funded under section 121 (American Indian Vocational Rehabilitation Services Program (AIVRS), if funded by the state), and a representative of

the state educational agency responsible for the education of students with disabilities under part B of the Individuals with Disabilities Education Act
- Allowed a council to have fewer than 15 members if it was in existence prior to the 1992 amendments to the Act
- Clarified that the director of the VR agency was a nonvoting member of the council
- Added a requirement that the appointing authority, to the greatest extent practicable, consider the extent to which minority populations were represented on the council
- Allowed the governor to delegate to the council the authority to fill vacancies on the council
- Removed the time limit on appointments for certain council members

In adding clarifications concerning council membership, the committee amendments specified that the representative of the Client Assistance Program and, if the state had one, the representative from the Native American Project funded under part C were excepted from the prohibition against council members serving more than two consecutive terms. This clarification was made in recognition of the limited size of the staff associated with many such programs and projects and the value of continuity in representation given the unique functions of these programs and projects. The committee was urged to assign the same exception status to the director of a state's parent information and training center, but declined this request. Such centers have employees, sponsors, parents assisted by the center, and volunteers, most of whom are parents or strong advocates for children with disabilities. By requiring parent centers to rotate their representatives on the SRC, as is required of most council members, the committee intended for such rotation to bring vitality and diversity to the council with regard to the needs of children with disabilities who may someday need VR services.

Regarding council functions, the committee amended the current law by (a) clarifying that the council should analyze and advise the VR agency regarding its performance in helping individuals with disabilities achieve employment outcomes; (b) specifying that, in partnership with the VR agency, the council should develop and review state goals and priorities, evaluate the effectiveness of the VR program, and submit reports of progress to the commissioner of the Rehabilitation Services Administration; (c) clarifying that the council should advise the VR agency regarding authorized activities and assist in the preparation of the state plan and amendments to the plan, applications, reports, needs assessments, and evaluations; (d) simplifying the scope of the council's analysis of the state VR program's effectiveness and consumer satisfaction with the state VR program and requiring the council to address individuals' employment outcomes and the availability of health and other employment benefits in connection with such employment outcomes; and (e) clarifying the council's functions related to coordination with other entities. The committee intended these amendments to further its goal of creating a consumer-oriented and consumer-driven VR system (Senate Committee on Labor and Human Resources, 1998, p. 26).

The finalized 1998 amendments focused on the growing population of Americans with disabilities, their disadvantaged status, and the goal of providing tools to them to achieve equality of opportunity, full inclusion and integration in society, employment, independent living, and economic and social self-sufficiency. The findings, purposes, and policy of the overall Act are stated in the legislation Section 100(a) as follows:

Findings

Congress finds that—

(1) millions of Americans have one or more physical or mental disabilities and the number of Americans with such disabilities is increasing;

(2) individuals with disabilities constitute one of the most disadvantaged groups in society;

(3) disability is a natural part of the human experience and in no way diminishes the right of individuals to—

    (A) live independently;

    (B) enjoy self-determination;

    (C) make choices;

    (D) contribute to society;

    (E) pursue meaningful careers; and

    (F) enjoy full inclusion and integration in the economic, political, social, cultural, and educational mainstream of American society;

(4) increased employment of individuals with disabilities can be achieved through implementation of statewide workforce investment systems under title I of the Workforce Investment Act of 1998 that provide meaningful and effective participation for individuals with disabilities in workforce investment activities and activities carried out under the vocational rehabilitation program established under title I, and through the provision of independent living services, support services, and meaningful opportunities for employment in integrated work settings through the provision of reasonable accommodations;

(5) individuals with disabilities continually encounter various forms of discrimination in such critical areas as employment, housing, public accommodations, education, transportation, communication, recreation, institutionalization, health services, voting, and public services; and

(6) the goals of the Nation properly include the goal of providing individuals with disabilities with the tools necessary to—

    (A) make informed choices and decisions; and

    (B) achieve equality of opportunity, full inclusion and integration in society, employment, independent living, and economic and social self-sufficiency, for such individuals.

Purpose

(1) to empower individuals with disabilities to maximize employment, economic self-sufficiency, independence, and inclusion and integration into society, through—

    (A) statewide workforce investment systems implemented in accordance with title I of the Workforce Investment Act of 1998 that include, as integral components, comprehensive and coordinated state-of-the-art programs of vocational rehabilitation;

    (B) independent living centers and services;

    (C) research;

    (D) training;

    (E) demonstration projects; and

    (F) the guarantee of equal opportunity; and

(2) to ensure that the Federal Government plays a leadership role in promoting the employment of individuals with disabilities, especially individuals with significant disabilities, and in assisting States and providers of services in fulfilling the

aspirations of such individuals with disabilities for meaningful and gainful employment and independent living.

Policy

(1) respect for individual dignity, personal responsibility, self-determination, and pursuit of meaningful careers, based on informed choice, of individuals with disabilities;

(2) respect for the privacy, rights, and equal access (including the use of accessible formats), of the individuals;

(3) inclusion, integration, and full participation of the individuals;

(4) support for the involvement of an individual's representative if an individual with a disability requests, desires, or needs such support; and

(5) support for individual and systemic advocacy and community involvement.

Title I (VR Services) Principles

Title I of the Act lists principles that the VR agencies must adhere to as they assess, plan, develop, and provide VR services to people with disabilities to achieve employment. These seven principles lay the foundation for how the public VR system works:

1. People with disabilities are presumed to be capable of work.
2. Employment opportunities should be in an integrated setting.
3. Consumers should have active participation and full partnership in the VR process.
4. Families and natural supports are important in the VR process.
5. The system must have qualified counselors, staff, and providers.
6. Consumers should have full participation and involvement with policy development and implementation.
7. Agencies must use accountability measures to facilitate program goals and objectives.

Considering Congress's findings and its establishment of the foregoing guiding principles, the Rehabilitation Act of 1973, as amended in 1998, was the monumental legislation that transformed the VR system from a medical model to a system requiring meaningful participation of the consumer in decision making and policy development and mandating the consumer-counselor partnership.

The 2014 Amendments and SRCs

SRC duties and functions were not significantly changed in Section 105 of the 2014 Amendments. However, there were significant changes of which SRCs need to be aware-

Congress sought to emphasize quality employment outcomes for persons with significant disabilities. This new emphasis was reflected in the addition of "integrated" to "competitive employment" and the removal of increased employment closures as a standard and indicator or a performance measure. Acceptable employment closures must be in jobs that are not segregated from others without disabilities. VR successful closures must now be employed in the 1st and 4th quarter after hire, not just 90 days.

2014 WIOA placed a greater emphasis on transition services for youth and students with disabilities. VR is now required to spend 15% from federal funds reserved in accordance with 361.65, and any funds made available from State, local, or private funding sources on pre-employment transition services (Pre-ETS) and to serve potentially eligible individuals.

Some other language changes included: "State Workforce Investment Board" changed to "State Workforce Development Board". "State Plan" was changed to "Vocational Rehabilitation portion of the Unified or Combined State Plan".

SRC Composition and Functions as Outlined in Section 105

The full text of Section 105, as amended under WIOA 2014, is as follows:

SEC. 105. State Rehabilitation Council
(a) ESTABLISHMENT-
(1) IN GENERAL.—Except as provided in section 101(a)(21)(A)(i), to be eligible to receive financial assistance under this title a State shall establish a State Rehabilitation Council (referred to in this section as the ''Council'') in accordance with this section.
(2) SEPARATE AGENCY FOR INDIVIDUALS WHO ARE BLIND.— A State that designates a State agency to administer the part of the State plan under which vocational rehabilitation services are provided for individuals who are blind under section 101(a)(2)(A)(i) may establish a separate Council in accordance with this section to perform the duties of such a Council with respect to such State agency.
(b) COMPOSITION AND APPOINTMENT.—
    (1) COMPOSITION
    (2) (A) IN GENERAL.—Except in the case of a separate Council established under subsection (a)(2), the Council shall be composed of—
(i) at least one representative of the Statewide Independent Living Council established under section 705, which representative may be the chairperson or other designee of the Council;
(ii) at least one representative of a parent training and information center established pursuant to section 671 of the Individuals with Disabilities Education Act;
(iii) at least one representative of the client assistance program established under section 112;
(iv) at least one qualified vocational rehabilitation counselor, with knowledge of and experience with vocational rehabilitation programs, who shall serve as an ex officio, nonvoting member of the Council if the counselor is an employee of the designated State agency;
(v) at least one representative of community rehabilitation program service providers;
(vi) four representatives of business, industry, and labor;
(vii) representatives of disability advocacy groups representing a cross section of—
(I) individuals with physical, cognitive, sensory, and mental disabilities; and
(II) individuals' representatives of individuals with disabilities who have difficulty in representing themselves or are unable due to their disabilities to represent themselves;
(viii) current or former applicants for, or recipients of, vocational rehabilitation services;
(ix) in a State in which one or more projects are funded under section 121, at least one representative of the directors of the projects located in such State;
(x) at least one representative of the State educational agency responsible for the public education of students with disabilities who are eligible to receive services under this title and part B of the Individuals with Disabilities Education Act; and
(xi) at least one representative of the State workforce development board.

(3) (B) SEPARATE COUNCIL.—In the case of a separate Council established under subsection (a)(2), the Council shall be composed of—

(i) at least one representative described in subparagraph (A)(i);

(ii) at least one representative described in subparagraph (A)(ii);

(iii) at least one representative described in subparagraph (A)(iii);

(iv) at least one vocational rehabilitation counselor described in subparagraph (A)(iv), who shall serve as described in such subparagraph;

(v) at least one representative described in subparagraph (A)(v);

(vi) four representatives described in subparagraph (A)(vi);

(vii) at least one representative of a disability advocacy group representing individuals who are blind;

(viii) at least one individual's representative, of an individual who—

(I) is an individual who is blind and has multiple disabilities; and

(II) has difficulty in representing himself or herself or is unable due to disabilities to represent himself or herself;

(ix) applicants or recipients described in subparagraph (A)(viii);

(x) in a State described in subparagraph (A)(ix), at least one representative described in such subparagraph;

(xi) at least one representative described in subparagraph (A)(x); and

(xii) at least one representative described in subparagraph (A)(xi).

(C) EXCEPTION.—In the case of a separate Council established under subsection (a)(2), any Council that is required by State law, as in effect on the date of enactment of the Rehabilitation Act Amendments of 1992, to have fewer than 15 members shall be deemed to be in compliance with subparagraph (B) if the Council—

(i) meets the requirements of subparagraph (B), other than the requirements of clauses (vi) and (ix) of such subparagraph; and

(ii) includes at least—

(I) one representative described in subparagraph (B)(vi); and

(II) one applicant or recipient described in subparagraph (B)(ix).

(2) EX OFFICIO MEMBER.—The Director of the designated State unit shall be an ex officio, nonvoting member of the Council.

(3) APPOINTMENT.—Members of the Council shall be appointed by the Governor or, in the case of a State that, under State law, vests authority for the administration of the activities carried out under this Act in an entity other than the Governor (such as one or more houses of the State legislature or an independent board), the chief officer of that entity. The appointing authority shall select members after soliciting recommendations from representatives of organizations representing a broad range of individuals with disabilities and organizations interested in individuals with disabilities. In selecting members, the appointing authority shall consider, to the greatest extent practicable, the extent to which minority populations are represented on the Council.

(4) QUALIFICATIONS.—

(A) IN GENERAL.—A majority of Council members shall be persons who are—

(i) individuals with disabilities described in section 7(20)(B); and

(ii) not employed by the designated State unit.

(B) SEPARATE COUNCIL.—In the case of a separate Council established under subsection (a)(2), a majority of Council members shall be persons who are—

(i) blind; and

(ii) not employed by the designated State unit.

(5) CHAIRPERSON.—

(A) IN GENERAL.—Except as provided in subparagraph (B), the Council shall select a chairperson from among the membership of the Council.

(B) DESIGNATION BY CHIEF EXECUTIVE OFFICER.—In States in which the chief executive officer does not have veto power pursuant to State law, the appointing authority described in paragraph (3) shall designate a member of the Council to serve as the chairperson of the Council or shall require the Council to so designate such a member.

(6) TERMS OF APPOINTMENT.—

(A) LENGTH OF TERM.—Each member of the Council shall serve for a term of not more than 3 years, except that—

(i) a member appointed to fill a vacancy occurring prior to the expiration of the term for which a predecessor was appointed, shall be appointed for the remainder of such term; and

(ii) the terms of service of the members initially appointed shall be (as specified by the appointing authority described in paragraph (3)) for such fewer number of years as will provide for the expiration of terms on a staggered basis.

(B) NUMBER OF TERMS.—No member of the Council, other than a representative described in clause (iii) or (ix) of paragraph (1)(A), or clause (iii) or (x) of paragraph (1)(B), may serve more than two consecutive full terms.

(7) VACANCIES.—

(A) IN GENERAL.—Except as provided in subparagraph (B), any vacancy occurring in the membership of the Council shall be filled in the same manner as the original appointment. The vacancy shall not affect the power of the remaining members to execute the duties of the Council.

(B) DELEGATION.—The appointing authority described in paragraph (3) may delegate the authority to fill such a vacancy to the remaining members of the Council after making the original appointment.

(c) FUNCTIONS OF COUNCIL.—The Council shall, after consulting with the State workforce development board—

(1) review, analyze, and advise the designated State unit regarding the performance of the responsibilities of the unit under this title, particularly responsibilities relating to—

(A) eligibility (including order of selection);

(B) the extent, scope, and effectiveness of services provided; and

(C) functions performed by State agencies that affect or that potentially affect the ability of individuals with disabilities in achieving employment outcomes under this title;

(2) in partnership with the designated State unit—

(A) develop, agree to, and review State goals and priorities in accordance with section 101(a)(15)(C); and

(B) evaluate the effectiveness of the vocational rehabilitation program and submit reports of progress to the Commissioner in accordance with section 101(a)(15)(E);

(3) advise the designated State agency and the designated State unit regarding activities authorized to be carried out under this title, and assist in the preparation of the State plan

and amendments to the plan, applications, reports, needs assessments, and evaluations required by this title;

(4) to the extent feasible, conduct a review and analysis of the effectiveness of, and consumer satisfaction with—

(A) the functions performed by the designated State agency;

(B) vocational rehabilitation services provided by State agencies and other public and private entities responsible for providing vocational rehabilitation services to individuals with disabilities under this Act; and

(C) employment outcomes achieved by eligible individuals receiving services under this title, including the availability of health and other employment benefits in connection with such employment outcomes;

(5) prepare and submit an annual report to the Governor and the Commissioner on the status of vocational rehabilitation programs operated within the State, and make the report available to the public;

(6) to avoid duplication of efforts and enhance the number of individuals served, coordinate activities with the activities of other councils within the State, including the Statewide Independent Living Council established under section 705, the advisory panel established under section 612(a)(20) of the Individuals with Disabilities Education Act, the State Council on Developmental Disabilities established under section 125 of the Developmental Disabilities Assistance and Bill of Rights Act of 2000, the State mental health planning council established under section 1914(a) of the Public Health Service Act (42 U.S.C. 300x– 3(a)) and the State workforce development board, and with the activities of entities carrying out programs under the Assistive Technology Act of 1998 (29 U.S.C. 3001 et seq.);

(7) provide for coordination and the establishment of working relationships between the designated State agency and the Statewide Independent Living Council and centers for independent living within the State; and

(8) perform such other functions, consistent with the purpose of this title, as the State Rehabilitation Council determines to be appropriate, that are comparable to the other functions performed by the Council.

(d) RESOURCES.—

(1) PLAN.—The Council shall prepare, in conjunction with the designated State unit, a plan for the provision of such resources, including such staff and other personnel, as may be necessary and sufficient to carry out the functions of the Council under this section. The resource plan shall, to the maximum extent possible, rely on the use of resources in existence during the period of implementation of the plan.

(2) RESOLUTION OF DISAGREEMENTS.—To the extent that there is a disagreement between the Council and the designated State unit in regard to the resources necessary to carry out the functions of the Council as set forth in this section, the disagreement shall be resolved by the Governor consistent with paragraph (1).

(3) SUPERVISION AND EVALUATION.—Each Council shall, consistent with State law, supervise and evaluate such staff and other personnel as may be necessary to carry out its functions under this section.

(4) PERSONNEL CONFLICT OF INTEREST.—While assisting the Council in carrying out its duties, staff and other personnel shall not be assigned duties by the designated

State unit or any other agency or office of the State, that would create a conflict of interest.

(e) CONFLICT OF INTEREST.—No member of the Council shall cast a vote on any matter that would provide direct financial benefit to the member or otherwise give the appearance of a conflict of interest under State law.

(f) MEETINGS.—The Council shall convene at least four meetings a year in such places as it determines to be necessary to conduct Council business and conduct such forums or hearings as the Council considers appropriate. The meetings, hearings, and forums shall be publicly announced. The meetings shall be open and accessible to the general public unless there is a valid reason for an executive session.

(g) COMPENSATION AND EXPENSES.—The Council may use funds allocated to the Council by the designated State unit under this title (except for funds appropriated to carry out the client assistance program under section 112 and funds reserved pursuant to section 110(c) to carry out part C) to reimburse members of the Council for reasonable and necessary expenses of attending Council meetings and performing Council duties (including child care and personal assistance services), and to pay compensation to a member of the Council, if such member is not employed or must forfeit wages from other employment, for each day the member is engaged in performing the duties of the Council.

(h) HEARINGS AND FORUMS.—The Council is authorized to hold such hearings and forums as the Council may determine to be necessary to carry out the duties of the Council.

29 U.S.C. 725

Other SRC Mandates in Title I

Throughout Title I, there are mandates for the state VR agency in reference to the SRC that parallel and expand on Section 105 as illustrated below:

- **Section 7(16):** SRC members cannot serve as an impartial hearing officer. (See Chapter 4 for further mandates for the impartial hearing officer and impartial due process hearings.)
- **Section 101(a)(15):** Every 3 years, VR and SRCs must jointly conduct a comprehensive needs assessment describing the rehabilitation needs of individuals with disabilities residing within the state- particularly the vocational rehabilitation needs of::
  - ➤ Individuals with disabilities, particularly individuals with the most significant disabilities (including their need for supported employment); minorities; those who have been unserved or underserved by VR; those who are served under other components of the Workforce Investment System; youth with disabilities and students with disabilities, including their need for pre employment transition or other transition services..
  - ➤ And the need to establish, develop, or improve community rehabilitation programs.
- **Section 101(a)(15)(C):** SRC and VR must jointly develop, agree to, and annually review the VR state plan goals and objectives.
- **Section 101(a)(15)(E):** SRC and VR must submit an annual joint report to the commissioner on the effectiveness of the VR program; the progress made in improving from the previous year; the extent to which goals were achieved, with strategies

contributing to goal achievement and factors that impeded success; and the assessment of performance on standards and indicators.

- **Section 101(a)(21)(A)(ii):** The state plan must provide for the following:
  - ➢ VR has an SRC that meets the criteria set forth in Section 105.
  - ➢ With the SRC, VR develops, agrees to, and reviews VR goals and priorities annually and submits annual progress reports.
  - ➢ VR regularly consults with the SRC on development, implementation, and revision of VR policies and procedures.
  - ➢ VR includes in the state plan, and any revision, a summary of SRC input; recommendations from the SRC annual report; a review and analysis of consumer satisfaction and other reports prepared by the SRC; and a response to SRC input and recommendations, including explanations for rejecting input or recommendations. In addition, VR transmits to the SRC all plans, reports, and other information on policies, practices, and procedures, as well as copies of due process hearings.
- **Section 101(a)(21)(B):** If the state has separate agencies for "general" and "blind," it may have one council or two councils.
- **Section 102(c)(8)(C)(d):** VR, in consultation with the SRC, must develop and implement written policies and procedures to enable each applicant to exercise informed choice throughout the VR process.
- **Section 107(a)(2)(G); (4)(C); (5):** In monitoring and reviewing VR, the commissioner shall consider information provided by the SRC under Section 105; conduct meetings with the SRC; examine areas identified by the public or through the SRC; and report on findings of the annual review or on onsite monitoring available to the SRC.

Legislative Process

Throughout this document, SRC mandates are referred to as both "Section 105" and as Section "361.16 and 361.17". Section 105 refers to the law. Sections 361.16 and 361.17 refer to the Code of Federal Regulations (CFR) that implement the law.

The Workforce Innovation and Opportunity Act (WIOA) is the overall legislation, of which the Rehabilitation Act is now Title IV. Within Title IV, we find Title 1- Vocational Rehabilitation Services. This is the section of the law that describes the VR program with which the SRC is mandated to partner. Therefore within Title 1, we find the SRC mandated section- "Section 105".

After the law is passed, there must be Regulations promulgated to implement the law. These Regulations address everything in the law and expand on the language to make it clear how to implement the mandates. The Regulations cannot contradict the law. The Rehabilitation Act Regulations are found in 34 CFR 361, and within these we find the SRC's- "Section 361.16 1nd 361.17".

The following chart illustrates this progression.

WIOA
(Workforce Innovation & Opportunity Act)
↓
Title IV of WIOA
(Rehabilitation Act)
↓
Title I of Title IV
(VR Services)
↓
Section 105 of Title I
(State Rehabilitation Council- SRC)
↓
CFR 361.16 & 361.17
(SRC Implementing Regulations)

Conclusion

Through the amendments of 1992 and 1998 Congress provided for greater consumer partnership. In particular, the 1998 amendments clearly stated the findings of Congress and defined the principles of the Rehabilitation Act and the principles for the conduct of business of Title I of the Act. The 1992 and 1998 amendments solidified the intent of Congress to involve consumers and the rehabilitation community as full partners in the public VR program. The 2014 WIOA emphasizes quality employment outcomes and transition services for youth and students with disabilities.

References

34 CFR § 361.17
https://www.govinfo.gov/content/pkg/CFR-2017-title34-vol2/xml/CFR-2017-title34-vol2-part361.xml
WIOA regulations
https://www.govinfo.gov/content/pkg/FR-2016-08-19/pdf/2016-15975.pdf
Text of WIOA
https://www.govinfo.gov/content/pkg/PLAW-113publ128/pdf/PLAW-113publ128.pdf

Chapter 2:
SRC Basics

This chapter provides the foundation for how State Rehabilitation Councils (SRCs) came into existence, based on the legal responsibilities detailed in chapter 1. The Rehabilitation Act as amended (the Act) provides SRC membership requirements through passages about composition, the appointment process, and terms of service. The leadership of each SRC greatly benefits by fully understanding these topics. This knowledge base adds significant value to the SRCs as they work toward achieving their federal mandates, since the leaders can be aware of pending vacancies due to term limits, areas of focus for recruitment, and ways to utilize the talents of each member in operationalizing the council's work plan.

Composition

Each SRC is expected to be the "consumer voice," and the statutory composition brings together important constituencies as detailed in Section 105 through 34 CFR (361.16 and 17) of the Rehabilitation Act (see chapter 1):

(1) **Composition**

    (A) **In general.** Except in the case of a separate Council established under subsection (a)(3), the Council shall be composed of at least 15 members, including-

        (i) at least one representative of the Statewide Independent Living Council who may be the chairperson or other designee of the Council;

        (ii) at least one representative of a parent training and information center established pursuant to section 682(a) of the Individuals with Disabilities Education Act;

        (iii) at least one representative of the Client Assistance Program (CAP) who must be the director of or other individual recommended by the CAP.

        (iv) at least one qualified vocational rehabilitation counselor, with knowledge of and experience with vocational rehabilitation programs, who serves as an ex officio, nonvoting member of the Council if the counselor is an employee of the designated State agency;

        (v) at least one representative of community rehabilitation program service providers;

        (vi) four representatives of business, industry, and labor;

        (vii) representatives of disability advocacy groups that represent a cross section of—

            (A) individuals with physical, cognitive, sensory, and mental disabilities; (In the case of a separate Blind agency Council, at least one representative of a disability advocacy group representing individuals who are blind); and

            (B) representatives of individuals with disabilities who have difficulty in representing themselves or are unable due to their disabilities to represent themselves. (In the case of a separate Blind agency council.at least one representative of an individual who is blind, has multiple disabilities, and has difficulty representing self or is unable due to disabilities to represent self);

        (viii) current or former applicants for, or recipients of, vocational rehabilitation services;

        (ix) in a State in which one or more projects are funded under section 121 of the Act (American Indian Vocational Rehabilitation Services), at least one representative of the directors of the projects in such state;

        (x) at least one representative of the State educational agency responsible for the public education of students with disabilities who are eligible to receive services under this title and part B of the Individuals with Disabilities Education Act;

(xi) at least one representative of the State workforce development board: and

(xii) the Director of the designated State unit shall be an ex officio, nonvoting member of the Council.

A majority of the Council members must be individuals with disabilities who meet the requirements of Section 361.5(c)(28) and are not employed by the designated State unit. In the case of a separate Blind agency Council, a majority of Council members must be individuals who are blind and not employed by the designated State unit.

The appointing authority must consider, to the greatest extent practicable, the extent to which minority populations are represented on the Council.

One SRC created a membership composition mandates chart to track the federal requirements for each member category (see chart in Appendix E) This document assists the executive committee in succession planning and the focus needed for recruitment of new members. SRCs have reported a wide variance in the size of their membership, from 15 to 32, with some states having as many as 14 ex officio members. Based on a survey conducted by an IRI Primary Study Group, the average membership size seems to be under 20. Although the SRC may not be in a situation to change the membership of its council, the provisions in the Act describe requirements to ensure that the SRC functions according to a group process. Diversity of membership was established to ensure that as the SRC works to review, analyze, and advise the vocational rehabilitation (VR) system, a plethora of opinions and knowledge about the VR system is present to ensure a broader perspective. At the same time, the challenge from this diversity in membership presents itself in keeping individual interests in check while focusing on improving VR performance and achieving employment outcomes. A critical aspect of the learning curve for SRC members is to fully understand their role and responsibilities in relationship to the mission of the council; this may be provided through orientation and ongoing training mechanisms, which are discussed later in this chapter.

Legal Basis for SRCs

Section 105 of the Act mandates that each state have an SRC, unless it has an independent commission as provided in section 101(a)(21)(A)(i). SRCs report that councils are established by the governor's executive order, through state boards of education, or by state statute. While it may not be necessary to have a legal document at the state level, an executive order offers several advantages, as it brings the legal basis to the local level with regard to the uniqueness found in each state or territory and may provide additional criteria for membership, the appointing authority, the management of vacancies, and the functioning of the SRC.

These documents usually contain language mirroring the requirements of section 105. If, however, they include provisions that run counter to these statutory provisions, the federal law takes precedence.

Organizational Variation

A variety of SRC organizational structures are in place across the country. Some function on their own with assistance from agency personnel, while others have their own staff who function autonomously from the agency. There are benefits to having dedicated staff, since appointees to councils are volunteers and have full lives outside of their SRC work responsibilities. SRCs with dedicated, autonomous staff have someone behind the scenes to organize and manage business meeting plans, facilitate effective communication and teamwork, schedule and assist at committee meetings, provide organizational history, and represent them at agency workgroups and/or partnership meetings when an SRC member is not available. When a staff person is available to take care of the daily business, SRC members can focus their time and attention on the review and analysis of data, which results in membership-driven input and recommendations to VR. If VR liaison staff are assigned to assist, the SRC should help to ensure that the council remains truly consumer driven. A number of states report that VR liaisons can and do function in a manner that allows the SRC to operate effectively.

Some SRCs report that they are successful without dedicated staff when they have a dedicated group of members who get all the work done.

Appointment and Terms of Service

Section 105 through 34 CFR (361.17) in the Rehabilitation Act provides specific detail regarding the time period and number of terms that SRC members can serve:

(A) Length of term

Each member of the Council shall serve for a term of not more than 3 years, except that—

(i) a member appointed to fill a vacancy occurring prior to the expiration of the term for which a predecessor was appointed, shall be appointed for the remainder of such term; and

(ii) the terms of service of the members initially appointed shall be (as specified by the appointing authority described in paragraph (3) for such fewer number of years as will provide for the expiration of terms on a staggered basis.

(B) Number of terms

No member of the Council, other than the CAP and 121 representatives who have no term limit, may serve more than two consecutive full terms.

As mandated in the Act, each member can serve no more than two consecutive terms, or 6 years. The terms should be staggered so that all member terms do not expire the same year. The Client Assistance Program and the 121 (Native American) VR project director positions have no term limits and are typically filled by the same individual over time. The term limit imposed for most members, however, leads to turnover that can negatively impact the council's functioning capacity for the long term.

Some SRCs report that most new members only begin to fully understand their roles and responsibilities after 2 years of service. This learning curve combined with the term limits presents a conundrum for SRCs, which must determine the best approach for the recruitment of members, expedite the appointment process so that vacancies do not occur, and then educate new members about the work of the council so they become involved, make a commitment, and are viable members who add value to the council.

As expected from the wide variety of SRC operational practices nationwide, the appointment process can vary greatly from state to state. For some councils, the governor chooses all members; in others, SRCs present a list of candidates to the governor's appointing authority, for consideration; in still others, SRCs request the members they want and receive the appointments. One of the biggest challenges reported by SRCs is the difficulty of receiving timely appointments, typically from governors. Numerous efforts have been made by SRC members and staff, VR agency staff, and even elected officials to expedite the process, with little success reported. Some SRCs have waited as long as 2 years for appointments to be made, even as their membership dwindles to less than the mandated categories, which diminishes the SRC's impact on the VR system. A few SRCs have reported the value they have realized from diligently working to establish an effective relationship with the appointments office staff through continually educating them about SRC responsibilities and member needs, maintaining communication, and showing appreciation for appointments.

Some council members, whose terms have expired, continue to attend council meetings, serve on committees, and participate in activities of the council even though they cannot vote nor be financially reimbursed. However, their experience of having served on the council for a number of years can be invaluable and their continued involvement in the council should be encouraged. This raises the question- can an individual whose term has expired be reappointed, and is there a time limit before they can be nominated for reappointment? The law does not address this issue. However, many state SRCs have established time frames, ranging from two months to a year, and made sure this is stated in their By-Laws.

Continuous Recruitment

As stated above, many SRCs are having issues with timely appointments from governor offices. Several strategies have already been identified in dealing with the appointment office. Another approach for dealing with this issue is to encourage persons nominated to attend council meetings and participate on committees and in other activities. By the time their appointment is finalized, they would be well oriented and have a clear understanding of the council's purpose and activities.

New SRC members should be continually recruited. One of the most effective models seems to be a multifaceted plan for recurrent outreach (by all members and staff having responsibility) to targeted populations with public relations materials created to showcase the work of the SRC, the time commitment involved, and the value to the public VR system as a result of service. Each SRC will benefit from an agreed-upon recruitment plan that is continuously in process. In keeping with the federal requirements, the plan must champion diversity by disability. Additionally, each SRC should determine the diversity present in its state as related to gender, race, ethnicity, sexual preference, etc., and include the characteristics in their plan.

Some SRCs have reported that having a committee dedicated to membership recruitment can address many of the ongoing challenges involved in recruiting new members. Unlike the more passive advisory role of traditional advisory councils, participation in SRCs involves completion of federal requirements that must be managed through the commitment of time by a volunteer membership. Many SRCs educate potential members prior to their appointment about the time commitment that is needed to be a member. In addition, many SRCs report that they inform potential members about the overarching SRC goal to review, analyze, and advise system wide issues of the VR program, rather than personal agenda matters. One state's recruitment packet includes a list of expected SRC member work responsibilities, such as quarterly in-person business meetings, teleconference committee meetings, agency workgroups, partner activities, and review of various informational documents via e-mail—activities that require an average of 8 to 10 hours per month.

Some SRCs interview potential members before recommending them for appointment. The interview is conducted by at least two members and a staff person, in a communication and physically accessible environment, with the dual goal of educating the appointee and gaining information about the individual. This allows the SRC to make an informed decision about the ongoing growth and development of its membership. An example of questions utilized by one SRC follows:

1. How did you hear about the SRC?
2. Please describe why you are interested in becoming a member of the SRC.
3. What do you see as the role of the SRC?
4. What strengths do you hope to bring to the council?
5. What other qualities, interests, etc. do you have that will enhance the SRC and our mission?
6. How do you handle situations in which you are the representative of a group and you don't personally believe or support a position of that group?
7. Will you be able to commit to the quarterly meeting and committee meeting time requirements?
8. After reviewing the SRC committee structure, what committees would you be interested in serving on?
9. Much of the SRC work is done through e-mail. Are you able to commit to responding promptly to e-mail communication?
10. The governor's office performs a background check on all applicants. Are you aware of any circumstances that might disqualify you from SRC membership?
11. Is there anything you would like to add about yourself or questions you may have about the SRC?

Each of these methods should result in potential members clearly understanding what is expected of them.

One critical aspect of the SRC's continuous recruitment efforts is a plan to establish a proactive relationship with the appointing authority in the state. One SRC reported that after a change in governors, the SRC chair, vice-chair, member, and staff person scheduled a meeting with the appointments specialist assigned to the council. The agenda for this meeting was focused on providing SRC 101 education for the new staff person along with discussions about the current status of the membership related to its recruitment efforts and vacancies. Another SRC reported that it invited the appointments staff person to a quarterly meeting every year, providing him with time on the agenda and recognizing him for work done on behalf of the SRC. One SRC asks its newly appointed members to send a thank you card to the governor and appointments staff to acknowledge their appreciation for the opportunity. Since many SRCs report that one of their challenges can be a lethargic appointments process, it makes good sense for the council leadership to cultivate a strong relationship with the appointing authority.

A common means of recruitment is to ask existing members to recommend coworkers and associates. One SRC has found that investing time into educating and informing agency staff about the roles and responsibilities of the SRC has led to names of potential members. A few SRCs reported that when attending conferences within their state, the council would host an exhibit and utilize the opportunity to recruit members from the population of attendees. These are effective methods but should not be the sole method of recruitment. Recruitment needs to take into account the geographical representation of the state or territory as well as gender, race, age, and disability.

A less-used strategy to recruit SRC members is for current SRC members to participate in other state disability councils. SRC members who join other councils have the opportunity to explain the VR program's successes and challenges and invite other councils to work with the SRC to improve VR services and outcomes. Personal interaction of SRC members with other councils is one way to put the SRC-VR partnership into practice. Collaboration with other councils raises awareness that employment is a high priority. Collaboration with other councils leads to successful efforts in educating public policymakers on the value of employing the individuals with disabilities whom VR serves, as well as that employment's positive impact on the state economy.

An alternative to membership on multiple councils is to have designated council members give presentations to other councils and disability organizations on the responsibilities of the SRC. This presentation provides the opportunity to seek their feedback for the comprehensive statewide needs assessment and state plan and to encourage them to consider membership in the SRC.

Of the categories of membership, councils have expressed the most difficulty recruiting business, industry, and labor representatives, as well as a member of the state Workforce Development Board. Some SRCs have strategically focused on the following potential members:

- Self-employed individuals who worked with VR to set up their business
- Employers recognized for diverse hiring practices
- Chamber of Commerce members
- Labor union leaders
- Randolph-Sheppard operators
- Members of the state or local chapter of the Society for Human Resource Management (see http://www.shrm.org/Communities/SHRMChapters/ProfessionalChapters/Pages/default.aspx#search)

Orientation

For SRC members to be valuable and effective partners with VR, they must develop a keen understanding of the role and function they play. A variety of SRC training practices exist; however, almost all SRCs agree that orientation and training of members should include several elements:

- The history of the public VR program
- Federal/state structure and partnership.
- Section 105 connection to the Rehabilitation Act and WIOA.
- The major provisions of the Rehabilitation Act of 1973, as amended
- The roles and responsibilities of the SRC as set forth in the Rehabilitation Act
- The vocational rehabilitation process
- The VR agency's policies and practices
- Visits to VR administrative and field offices and community rehabilitation programs
  * A SRC Orientation 101 package is available on the NCSRC website- www.ncsrc.net

This knowledge ensures that the SRC complies with the structure, function, and activities of the Act and follows its philosophy and intent. Having members who are well trained and educated benefits not only the state VR program and director, but more importantly the eligible individuals with disabilities who receive services.

Training on the VR process helps members provide more meaningful advice to the state agency. Such training should include but not be limited to the following areas:

- The Rehabilitation Act
- The VR process: application, pre employment transition services, eligibility, ineligibility, order of selection, the individualized plan for employment, informed consumer choice,

21

financial needs test, comparable benefits, scope of services, case closure, postemployment services

- Client rights and responsibilities within the VR process; the role of the Client Assistance Program; the option for mediation and the appeals process

Some SRCs provide training individually for members as they are appointed by the governor; others provide training in a small group setting when several new members are appointed. Still other SRCs offer a member handbook (see example in Appendix E) to supplement the individual or group training/orientation. Another option is to combine training for new SRC members with training for new counselors. These examples are in no way exhaustive.

Involving the state director, VR staff, and other key leaders in training has many benefits. The interaction between these individuals and the SRC members builds a bond and feeling of trust; it allows them to get to know each other and creates an atmosphere of open communication.

In addition to training and ongoing information about the VR service system, many SRCs report that members have benefitted from training that strengthens teamwork. Topics for trainings include Robert's Rules of Order, consensus agendas, disability awareness and history, Social Security benefits, teambuilding, leadership, effective communication strategies, strategic plan writing, and strategies for educating and informing the state legislature and Congress. It is apparent that as many SRCs engage in their federal responsibilities, they recognize the need for training that will augment their capacity to be effective leaders for the people being served by the VR agency.

Some SRCs have reported that VR staff do not understand the role and function of the SRC. In an effort to remedy this situation, many SRCs make presentations at new counselor training or at other staff training sessions. One council sends a letter of welcome to each new VR agency staff person and includes information about the role, responsibilities, and actions of the SRC. Another council incorporates staff presentations into its business meeting agenda and invites local staff to join them at lunch, so that members and staff can engage in dialogue for each other's benefit. Still another SRC has stressed the importance of understanding a day in the life of the front-line field staff, including their successes and barriers. This information serves the SRC in better focusing on system change efforts. Consumers benefit when staff receive what they need to be effective.

Ongoing Training

In a survey conducted by the IRI Study Group for the 2014 IRI, "SRC/VR Partnership" many respondents indicated that ongoing training opportunities were provided and typically designed by their SRC. They indicated a variety of ways that they engage in ongoing training:

- Holding an annual multiday retreat focused on the creation or review of a multiple-year strategic plan. The plans are described as a critical tool utilized by the SRCs to conduct their business throughout the year, with annual reviews of the progress made and identification of any barriers faced by the membership. Added benefits include members getting to better know each other and identifying special individual talents.
- Holding an annual 1-day retreat for the executive committee to consider how their leadership could augment the ongoing growth and development of the membership.

- Having a type of "in-service day" the day before the business meeting, incorporating time for committees to meet and for information to be offered about emerging issues, VR system updates, and/or other topics of interest to provide continual education for the members.
- Offering selected elements of the training to the entire SRC yearly to refresh knowledge of members' role in development and evaluation of the VR portion of the unified or combined state plan (SP). Breakout sessions could be offered for newer members.
- Setting aside a portion of the business meeting agenda for some type of educational opportunity to further inform the membership.
- Encouraging attendance at related conferences and training.

Ongoing training topics could include, but are not limited to:
- The Rehabilitation Act
- The VR process
- Pre employment transition services
- Order of selection for services
- Consumer informed choice
- The Unified or Combined State Plan (SP)
- Cooperative agreements
- Consumer satisfaction survey
- Comprehensive Statewide Needs Assessment
- Performance indicators
- Match and maintenance of effort
- Role of community rehabilitation programs
- Management information systems

These training opportunities share a common factor, in that SRCs depend on outside facilitators, guest speakers, and VR staff to complete the agendas. Even in dire economic times, SRCs recognize the benefit of having face-to-face planning sessions so they can be kept abreast of the current challenges of the VR agency and can reach consensus on any adjustments needed to the strategic plan and the action steps needed toward achieving the federal mandates.

Role of the Chair and Vice Chair

For the SRC to be a true partner with the state VR agency, the chair should have mutual ongoing communication with the state VR director. The development of that relationship is critical, as the SRC partners with VR to implement the provisions of the approved SP. Information from the VR is necessary for the SRC to be able to fulfill its mandate. When working in close collaboration with the state agency and state director, the chair should utilize this relationship as the agency formulates its work plans and initiatives. A strong collaboration and relationship between the SRC and VR ensures that eligible individuals with disabilities seeking VR services have all the resources and support they need to achieve their goals, while also ensuring that the state VR program is effective, efficient, and in compliance with federal statutes and regulations. In the federal regulations, the selection of the chair is described as follows:

(d) Chairperson
   (1) The chairperson must be selected by the members of the Council from among the voting members of the Council, subject to the veto power of the Governor; or

(2) In States in which the Governor does not have veto power pursuant to State law, the appointing authority described in paragraph (a)(1) of this section must designate a member of the Council to serve as the chairperson of the Council or must require the Council to designate a member to serve as chairperson.

SRC chairs who are proactive and substantially involved in performing council functions are improving agency performance. Effective chairs should be able to collaborate with a number of entities and personnel and to serve as the "point person" for the SRC in a variety of arenas. Each SRC has the discretion to delineate the specific roles and responsibilities of the chair, as long as it complies with the federal statute and the state's policies and rules.

Though not mandated in the law, each SRC's leadership structure may benefit from having a member serve as the vice-chair. The councils that report having this position as part of their executive committee indicated that it provides great benefit to the membership. A vice-chair is presented with the opportunity to step into the role of chair during any absence, as well as being mentored by the chair on responsibilities that enhance the workings of the SRC. This member should provide continuity, history, relationships with agency staff, a knowledge base of the federal requirements, and the efforts needed to guide the membership toward successful outcomes. In one state, the vice-chair is responsible for the preparation of the Annual Report.

Some SRCs have found it useful to create an annual SRC activity calendar, which leadership can use to direct the work of the council. An example of 2 months of a calendar utilized in one state is presented below.

October (beginning of fiscal year for agency)
- Gather agency and SRC accomplishments and challenges for annual report (due date December 30th)
- Establish state plan ad hoc committee and schedule initial meeting by December 1st
- Hold committee meetings
- Meet with state director, chair, vice-chair, and agency liaison staff

November
- Hold quarterly business meeting
- Hold committee meetings
- Hold executive committee meeting (follow up from business meeting)

Committees

Most SRCs have reported that their 15- to 32-member councils have a "lead" work team, or executive committee, consisting of five to six members and that the composition of officers is varied. Many report that their executive committee is composed of a chair, vice-chair, and members at large. Others have added a treasurer, secretary, past chair, or parliamentarian or have included the state director as an ex officio member of the executive committee.

Over the course of years since the SRCs were statutorily established, most SRCs have found that in order to be effective and relevant, a committee structure facilitated the work of the SRC.

Committees may be organized in a variety of ways. A committee structure allows members to break the work of the SRC into smaller and focused segments. This approach allows the committee to address issues in depth. Committees can communicate and work outside of business meetings and report back to the membership at a later date.

The number of committees an SRC might form varies. The involvement of committee members is essential to the productivity of SRC meetings. Effective committees bring all SRC members together to conduct the vital work of the council. Through these interactions, the synergy is created to bring varied and collective opinions together for the improvement of the VR program. The success of the committee often depends on the leadership provided by the chair.

Some SRCs report that each member of the executive committee is expected to serve as the chair for a committee, while others have members who volunteer to serve in this capacity. Each committee should reach consensus regarding the commitment needed by each member to ensure the completion of the work plan. It should be noted, that SRCs may supplement committee membership with non SRC members to broaden input into the discussions and the work of the SRC. SRC- created committees are not required to be comprised solely of SRC members. Many SRCs have used this method to recruit new members and broaden the SRC's outreach and visibility in the state. This is a way to introduce the SRC and its work in the state.

An effective SRC committee structure is necessary if the SRC is to be an effective partner with the State VR Agency. SRC members need to understand the challenges and successes of the Agency in order to provide the Agency with balanced and astute input into the issues which are facing the Public VR Program and individuals with disabilities in the state.

SRCs with active and substantive committees are absolutely necessary to the overall success of the councils in achieving the statute's mandates, and to the success of the state agencies. The SRC is a vital resource to the state agency and as such should be involved in the substantive discussions of the agency relative to program design and service delivery. This can be done through the work of the SRC committees.

Each SRC reported a committee structure designed for specific work tasks (e.g., state plan, consumer satisfaction) or themes (e.g., financial, service delivery effectiveness, public policy). Promising practices have been reported by SRCs that have established a strategic plan that mirrors each of the responsibilities in the Act. The following cycle has been utilized by some SRCs to educate members about the importance of committee work and outcomes.

- Education is offered about the Act, Section 105-SRC.
- The SRC creates a work plan to achieve mandates.
- A committee structure is designed and implemented.
- Committees design their work plans.
- Committees complete their work tasks for review and possible action by the full membership.
- Accomplishments are reviewed to determine the achievement of SRC mandates.

The implementation of this cyclical pattern serves as a system of checks and balances for the SRC.

The council work plan is typically designed to follow the fiscal year of the agency and has a goal with related activities/outcomes, which are assigned to the appropriate committee. Such a relationship is crucial to the success of the council and the agency partnership. Councils report that their committees typically meet monthly via teleconference, in addition to meeting face-to-face in conjunction with the business meeting schedule. During the course of the year, a committee may bring an action item or recommendation for membership consideration. On an annual basis, the committees summarize their accomplishments and provide a report to the full membership. This type of structure provides a twofold benefit for the SRC: (1) the entire membership is aware of and educated about the work of each committee and (2) the SRC can utilize the information to conduct an annual self-evaluation to determine successes and/or challenges in achieving the federal mandates.

Summary and Recommendations

Section 105 of the Act identifies the requirements for the SRC membership. The clearly defined categories of individuals who must be appointed to the SRC, along with a full membership complement of not less than 15 members, serve as the foundation for each council. The most critical membership requirement is the assurance that the majority of members will be people with disabilities. This ensures that the council is driven by a "consumer voice." Though not required by law, the best practice is for the SRC to further expand membership by considering factors such as race, ethnicity, culture, language, and other areas of diversity present in its state.

Employer involvement is both mandated and critical. Special efforts should be considered to recruit representation from business, industry, labor, and the State Workforce Development Board.

To support continuously evolving membership on SRCs, the Act mandates that appointments be made on a rotating basis. This dynamic results in the SRC having some members who are well versed about the SRC-VR partnership while newer members rotate on and bring new and fresh ideas.

The SRC chair, along with executive committee members, supports planning in two critical areas. The first area relates to membership: member recruitment, timely appointments to the council, and member turnover. The second area relates to the federal requirements, where the executive committee members can provide guidance, insight, commitment, and passion to encourage the SRC-VR partnership in the creation and implementation of a strategic work plan. The executive committee can also implement a plan for self-evaluation so that the members can celebrate their successes and plan accordingly for any challenges faced.

As SRCs increase their knowledge about VR and the federal VR regulations, members will greatly benefit from ongoing training opportunities. Training can be focused on emerging and/or current VR issues or on professional development needs. Each SRC should recognize and plan for training through a variety of modalities.

There is wide variance in how SRCs are organized and operate. Staff support for SRCs certainly varies from state to state. SRCs should have meaningful discussions about their need for staff and how this complement to the federal requirements can add value to their outcomes. Dedicated staff adds continuity and stability to SRCs, enhancing the development of the membership and assuring the maintenance of the SRCs' records, work efforts, and annual calendar.

References

Rehabilitation Act Amendments of 1973, as amended by WIOA 2014.
Workforce Innovation and Opportunity Act of 2014, Pub. L. No. 113-128 (7/22/2014)

Chapter 3:
SRC Business Practices

For a State Rehabilitation Council (SRC) to be a strong partner with vocational rehabilitation (VR), it needs sound business practices that include basic principles of partnership. Given the term limits of council members and change in VR administrators, business practices that incorporate partnership principles can help to sustain the SRC-VR partnership.

Developing a Mission Statement

A council mission statement should be succinct, avoid jargon, and define the fundamental purpose for the council's existence. The mission statement should provide the basis for evaluating the success of the council. It should state what the council wants to accomplish rather than how. Table 3-1 below provides examples of mission statements. Additional samples of mission statements can be obtained through links to individual state SRCs on the National Coalition of State Rehabilitation Councils (NCSRC) website (www.NCSRC.net).

Table 3-1
Sample Mission Statements

Source	Statement
Maine	The Mission of the State Rehabilitation Council is to partner with the Division of Vocational Rehabilitation in the development of state goals, priorities, policy, and practice, and to review and analyze the division's results and performance in support of securing and maintaining employment, through a process of informed choice, for individuals with disabilities.
Minnesota	Empower Minnesotans with disabilities to achieve their goals for employment, independent living, and community integration.
Mississippi	It is the express mission of the State of Mississippi Rehabilitation Council to ensure that Mississippians with disabilities have a strong role in shaping the VR program of the Mississippi Department of Rehabilitation Services.
Oklahoma	The Mission of the Oklahoma Rehabilitation Council is to facilitate consumer education and empowerment, to assure services are of high quality, and lead to employment of individuals with disabilities in the State of Oklahoma.
Wyoming	The Wyoming State Rehabilitation Council's mission is to review, analyze and advise the Division of Vocational Rehabilitation in the delivery of effective rehabilitation services which lead to employment for individuals with disabilities and, in partnership with the Division of Vocational Rehabilitation, advance the use of resources necessary to promote the independence of Wyoming's citizens with disabilities.

Scheduling Meetings

SRC meetings must be held at least four times a year, be publicly announced, and be open and accessible to the public unless there is a valid reason for an executive session. In addition, meetings may consist of hearings and forums as deemed necessary by the SRC.

Councils need to follow the laws of their state in relation to meeting documents and access. Sunshine laws govern public access to governmental records, which include the bylaws, reports, and minutes of SRC meetings. State open meeting laws govern public access to governmental meetings. (See a listing at http://sunshinereview.org/index.php/ State_sunshine_laws.)

Many other factors should be considered when scheduling meetings for a statewide council and its subcommittees. Some considerations include the size and geography of the state, population centers, availability of technology and remote conferencing options, and travel methods and routes. If members are traveling long distances, it sometimes makes more sense to schedule longer meetings to make the travel more worthwhile. Some SRCs indicate that it is easier to recruit members from private business if an evening format is utilized. There is no one right way to create meeting schedules that best meet the needs of diverse states.

A 2010 survey of SRCs asked how often meetings were held and for how long. The results are shown in Table 3-2. As the table indicates, most councils held four meetings a year, while five held monthly meetings. Councils meeting frequently met for a few hours or used teleconference or videoconference technology. Seventeen councils noted that they met in the same location for each meeting. Twenty-three councils rotated the location of their meetings throughout the year. The Act allows flexibility so SRCs can schedule meetings to balance the demands of time, travel, and council workload.

Table 3-2
Number and Length of Full SRC Meetings

Variable	No. of SRCs
Meetings per year (n)	
4	35
5	2
6	6
10	2
12	5
Length of each meeting (days)	
<0.5	6
0.5	13
1	18
1.5	7
2	2
3	2

Facilitating Effective Meetings and Council Communication

For both the full council and committee meetings, effective organization is critical to the function and outcome of the SRC, as is the full participation of all of the members. Keeping and disseminating minutes of the meetings is necessary for cohesiveness and is essential for keeping everything on track and moving forward. Setting a calendar annually and sending regular reminders help to ensure that busy council members set aside the necessary time to devote to council activities. Centralizing communication is also very helpful in engaging council members. Some councils post communication in a central location, such as a website, and some use a Yahoo or Google group for discussion. Provision of reasonable accommodations is a critical element for council meetings. Typically, council meeting accommodations include appropriate interpreters, handouts in alternate formats, and adaptive transportation assistance. Some SRCs have rules that no written handouts are circulated unless alternate formats are offered. Attention to these inclusive principles ensures maximum participation from all groups.

Establishing Committee Structure and Duties

Setting up the committee structure to carry out council responsibilities is one of the first tasks of SRCs. Committee structure is typically identified in bylaws, work plans, and annual reports. The partnership with VR is an important consideration, since a council may want to establish a committee structure that complements VR agency work groups. SRCs may also elect to change their committee structure for various reasons, such as unequal distribution of work for the committees, too many committees for staffing purposes, or too few committees leading to less participation by members.

Each council's committee structure is intended to be stable enough to ensure consistency yet flexible enough to respond to its state's rehabilitation needs. Both temporary and permanent committees can be created to respond to specific issues that arise in each state. Maryland's SRC created a new standing committee to advise its Office of Blindness and Vision Services. Maryland had set out to improve service delivery for this specific population and in doing so created a separate office of its combined VR program. To ensure that significant progress was made with targeted outcomes, a new committee was created, composed of both SRC and non-SRC members, in an effort to ensure the council was as informed as possible from this community.

Involving SRC and non-SRC members on ad hoc committees is a common strategy councils use to more fully inform their work. Ad hoc committee members may join the SRC's efforts because of specific expertise or interests. These committee members, who are not governor appointed, are not asked to give the same time commitment as a full member and are not given voting privileges. Ad hoc committee members might be involved in time-limited tasks, such as providing input into the needs assessment, or their involvement might be ongoing. Some SRCs attempt to recruit and prepare ad hoc committee members for full membership as other members rotate off the council. Their input and participation is very valuable to SRC committees.

Table 3-3 provides some examples of different states' committee structures.

Table 3-3
Sample Committee Structures

State	Committees
Maryland	Executive Committee: Oversees SRC activities
	Blindness and Vision Services Committee: For the Office for Blindness and Vision Services, assists in the development of planning activities; participates in policy development; assists with the comprehensive statewide needs assessment, program evaluation, comprehensive system of personnel development, and priority and standing objectives; reviews and monitors the grant for independent living services for older individuals; assesses consumer satisfaction
	Employment and Career Development Committee: Develops innovative projects related to employment outcomes; advises VR regarding enhancement of relationships with employers; assists in marketing and outreach to employers; advises regarding programs, focus, and performance of the Workforce and Technology Center
	Membership and Resources Committee: Monitors council composition; oversees recruitment; facilitates the appointment process; coordinates orientation of new members; develops the council budget; and ensures coordination with other councils
	Policy and Planning Committee: Assists in the development of the state plan; partners with VR with the annual public meetings; assists in the review of the comprehensive system of personnel development; and participates in the development and review of the triennial comprehensive statewide needs assessment
	Public Relations and Quality Assurance Committee: Develops and distributes public information materials and the annual report; provides recommendations related to information/data collection; reviews Client Assistance Program, mediation, and appeals reports; and coordinates legislative and advocacy activities

State	Committees
New York	Executive Committee: Provides leadership; assigns issues to standing committees; develops linkages with the business community; ensures that council work is done collaboratively; provides informational materials about the council; educates legislators, the business community, and other stakeholders regarding VR funding, legislation, and employment opportunities Membership Committee: Facilitates the recruitment and retention of SRC members; manages orientation and mentoring of new members; prepares nominations of new SRC members to the Board of Regents Quality Assurance and Improvement Committee: Reviews extent, scope, and effectiveness of VR services; conducts triennial statewide needs assessment; assesses consumer satisfaction Workforce Development Committee: Provides recommendations regarding state equal employment outcomes; reviews extent, scope, and effectiveness of employment and marketing services; develops partnerships with employers; reviews transition and school to work issues; jointly approves impartial hearing officers Policy, Procedures, and State Plan Committee: Helps prepare the state plan; advises regarding goals, policies, priorities, legislation, and postsecondary issues; identifies economic and other barriers that prevent the VR agency from serving larger numbers of people with disabilities

Retaining Active Members

How can we retain active members? Many SRCs have expressed the frustration, "They were so energized when they joined the council. What happened?" As council chairs and staff have discussed retaining active members, some common strategies have emerged:

Commit time to orientation and getting to know the interests and abilities of council members so committee assignments utilize those interests and abilities.

Review orientation materials at meetings to reinvigorate members to think about their role and responsibilities.

Share information about the National Coalition of State Rehabilitation Councils and its website (www.ncsrc.net) to motivate those interested in a national perspective.

Give ample opportunity at council meetings as well as committee meetings for input from members on what needs to be done and what is important.

Send council members to conferences of the National Coalition of State Rehabilitation Councils, Council of State Administrators of Vocational Rehabilitation, and National Council of State Agencies for the Blind for leadership development.

Send council members to professional development activities provided by the Rehabilitation Services Administration, National Coalition of State Rehabilitation Councils and VR to encourage more in-depth knowledge of the Act and its VR programs and services.

If an SRC is having difficulty recruiting or retaining active members, the VR administrator can play a key role in strengthening the council and the partnership. The VR agency has access to stakeholders and partners interested in the success of the VR program. The

VR agency can disseminate information about the council and its valued role, which can be a strong recruitment tool to draw in active members.

Developing Bylaws

It is important for SRCs to have structure independent from the VR agency such as bylaws, policies/procedures, or guidelines. Although an SRC may not be a 501©(3), bylaws still provide members and stakeholders clear expectations for the function of the council. Bylaws are rules adopted by the organization, in many cases amended over time, to define and direct the organization's internal structure (American Society of Association Executives, 2007). Some SRCs use other terms such as guidelines or guiding principles, but for the purpose of this section the term bylaws is utilized.

Bylaws can vary from one organization to another, yet at a minimum an SRC's bylaws should address the roles and responsibilities of the SRC and should concur with Part 361 of the federal regulations. Bylaws must not violate or attempt to override state or federal law. According to the American Society of Association Executives (2007), bylaws should be "neither so specific as to require frequent amending, nor so vague as to create uncertainty." A sample outline for the bylaws, with comments, is provided in Table 3-4.

Table 3-4
Suggested sections to be Included in SRC Bylaws

Section	Comment
1. Council purpose/function	Mission statements are typically broad to encompass the various activities the SRC will undertake over time. Examples of mission statements are found in the beginning of this chapter.
2. Appointment—composition of membership a. Vacancies	At a minimum, membership must include those entities mandated in federal regulation 361.17. The bylaws should also address vacancies and recruiting members based on the required composition of the council.
3. Membership a. Terms of appointments b. Officers/duties/terms c. Voting/nonvoting (ex officio) d. Removal of members e. Members' responsibilities/ standards	The Act provides for appointment terms of 3 years with no more than two consecutive terms, with several exceptions. This requirement can also be reflected in the bylaws. In addition to outlining the term limits for members, the Act mandates that membership terms be staggered so that SRCs do not have too many new members at one time. The bylaws should identify members who can vote and those who cannot, who are referred to "ex officio" members. Other subsections within membership could include the election of officers, their terms, and their titles and duties.
4. Conflict of interest a. Cannot vote on an issue in which the member would financially benefit b. Contribute field of expertise and avoid	Bylaws should provide guidance under circumstances when a conflict of interest may arise. At a minimum it must indicate that a member cannot vote on any matter that would provide a direct financial benefit to himself or herself or otherwise give the appearance of a conflict of interest under state law .

Section	Comment
personal platform	Additionally, since the required composition of the SRC membership is designed to contribute to the overall mission based on field of expertise and personal experience, it could be helpful to have a general statement about the importance of avoiding a personal platform.
5. Meetings a. Frequency b. Location c. Meeting structure d. Governing rules e. Compensation/expenses f. Accessibility g. Electronic participation h. Public meeting standards to comply with state law	SRCs are required to hold open public meetings at least four times a year. Each state has a great deal of flexibility as to where, when, and how long the meetings are held. Again, it is helpful if the bylaws give direction without being too prescriptive. For example, the bylaws should not state that the SRC will meet the third Thursday in January, April, July, and October, which could invalidate a quarterly meeting if circumstances required a change. Instead, it could state that at the last meeting of each year the council will determine the meeting dates and locations for the next year. The bylaws can also outline the structure in which the business will be conducted during the meeting, such as utilizing Robert's Rules of Order or a consensus model. A review of the state's open meeting laws could be provided in this section of the bylaws. Other general information for the meeting section could include compensation to members and/or reimbursement of expenses for members who attend meetings; the use of current and future technology for meeting and voting, which would allow for greater participation; and the ways the SRC intends to ensure that meetings are both physically and programmatically accessible to members and the public. Accessibility applies not only to the meeting place but also to the meeting materials and electronic information.
6. Quorum a. Establish a procedure: number of members vs. percentage of members b. Track eligibility to vote c. Voting procedure	It is best if the bylaws don't give an exact membership number to determine if a quorum exists, since those numbers can vary over time. Instead, use some type of percentage of voting members to ensure there are enough people present to conduct a comprehensive meeting. It is important to maintain a list of members who are eligible to vote and those that should not vote, either because they are ex officio members or have a conflict of interest on the matter. Bylaws can also provide guidance on voting procedures, by ballot, voice, or under certain circumstances electronically.
7. Organizational structure a. Fiscal year b. Resources i. Staff/responsibility of supervision	Among general organizational issues, the fiscal year for the SRC could be stated, such as calendar year, the state's fiscal year, or the federal fiscal year. It can be determined based on any 12-month cycle, but it should make the most sense for the business to be conducted. A section on resources could include staffing, fiscal management, and the annual

Section	Comment

ii. Finances
c. Committee structure
  i. Responsibilities/
    authorities
  ii. Ad hoc committee
    creation/dissolution
	development of a resource plan and/or contracting. How an SRC should resolve a dispute with the VR agency over a resource plan should also be discussed. Staffing is a critical area to an organization; bylaws should outline the overall duties of the staff and how staff, particularly those employed by the VR agency, avoid conflict of interest in other duties performed by the state. Federal regulation states that the SRC must supervise and evaluate the performance of the staff, and therefore should be outlined in the bylaws. The organizational section could also set up the structure of committees. It may be better to only name a few (two to four) standing committees and allow for ad hoc committees as needed. This provides the SRC flexibility to address pressing needs that cannot be predicted. Allowing for committees to come and go adds flexibility to effectively carry out council functions.

8. Amendment of bylaws	

In addition to bylaws, the SRC may want to develop policies or standard operational procedures. Bylaws provide the "why" of the organization, whereas policies and procedures provide the "how." Policies can explain the day-to-day responsibilities and activities of the staff and members.

The passage of WIOA led to updated regulations on the SRC role. An SRC should compare their current by-laws to determine if any updates are needed. An NCSRC analysis of the changes is included in Appendix C of this document.

Developing a Resource Plan

Federal regulation 361.17(i) requires SRCs to prepare a resource plan in conjunction with VR that provides resources, including funding, staff and personnel, and in-kind contributions, that are necessary to carry out SRC functions. The VR agency funds used for SRC operation should be identified as Administrative costs (361.5 (2)(v). All funds must flow through the VR agency to the SRC, which in turn must maintain some type of fiscal accountability for the use of the funds. The resource plan should include VR resources already in existence. In terms of personnel, the structure for staffing an SRC may differ from state to state; some VR agencies contract with an outside entity for staff to oversee the SRC day-to-day operations, while other states provide internal staff to support the activities of the council. In either case, the resource plan should reflect the level of funding that the VR agency will provide to the SRC.

Councils need to consider travel costs and mandated approval directives when arranging council meetings and member attendance at other functions. While a council needs to have the resources to perform their mandated functions, they also need to be good stewards of the taxpayer funds.

Written annual Prior Approval to RSA for SRC member out of state travel is no longer required. RSA granted such approval to states effective November 2019.

Below is an example of various categories for budget line items. SRCs, in partnership with VR, will need to determine their own budget categories. Certain categories may be listed with a projected cost yet be provided in kind to the SRC, while other categories will have an actual cost that will be directly expended based on resource plan decisions, such as travel expenses for staff and members.

Suggested Categories of Budget Items

Salary
Program manager
Administrative assistant
Fringe benefits
Administration
Audit/financial review
Information technology system support
Accommodations
Office
Supplies
Postage
Printing
Miscellaneous
Travel
Travel nonemployees
Travel staff expenses
Registration
Activities
Meetings and public hearings
Consumer satisfaction
Annual report/marketing materials
Conferences Training
Occupancy
Rent
Electronic telecommunications
Utilities
Equipment rental
Liability insurance
Fiscal agent fee

Summary

This chapter has presented an overview of the business practices an SRC needs to function as an effective partner despite changes in membership and changes in VR agency leadership. The business practices can be revised to meet the changing demands of the council. The VR agency can play an important role, providing expertise and information, so the SRC can tailor the business practices to the needs of both the SRC and the VR agency.

References

American Society of Association Executives. (2007). Bylaws. In Associapedia. Retrieved from http://www.asaecenter.org/wiki/?page=Bylaws

Chapter 4:
Implementation of Responsibilities

This chapter examines how State Rehabilitation Councils (SRCs) fulfill their mandated responsibilities found in the Rehabilitation Act, primarily in Section 105 through 34 CFR (361.17). The discussion will address information needed to fulfill the SRC role to "review, analyze, and advise" the vocational rehabilitation (VR) agency, consider an order of selection for services (OOS), work with the VR agency in development and review of the State Plan, provide input to the comprehensive system of personnel development, evaluate consumer satisfaction, facilitate public participation, select impartial hearing officers, and address advocacy issues.

Performance Evaluation: "Review, Analyze and Advise"

The SRC mandate to *review, analyze, and advise* VR agencies is a key obligation. Councils have a duty to review, analyze, and advise the state agency on "eligibility (including order of selection for services (OOS); the extent, scope, and effectiveness of services provided; and functions performed by state agencies that affect or potentially affect the ability of individuals with disabilities in achieving employment outcomes." The challenge for councils to effectively fulfill this duty is considerable, for several reasons:

- Council members are volunteers, with other full-time employment or responsibilities.
- Council members serve only one or two 3-year terms.
- Council members generally represent other disciplines and don't have the specific, detailed knowledge of the Rehabilitation Act and VR program needed to meet the obligations under the Act.
- Councils meet quarterly, some a bit more often, necessitating a very efficient use of time.
- Councils have responsibilities in addition to the duty to review, analyze, and advise, which build on this function. These responsibilities include effective evaluation of the VR agency; development of the state plan and state goals and priorities; consumer satisfaction; and the statewide needs assessment.

The accomplishment of the duty to review, analyze, and advise, within the timeframe of quarterly or periodic meetings, requires that councils have access to comprehensive data and information in a timely fashion. Without access to meaningful reports and statistics, the council cannot provide effective analysis or advice. The VR agency is responsible, as a partner of the council, to provide the information, data, and reports. Every VR agency produces extensive amounts of data on a regular basis. The selected reports and information to be provided to the SRC should be timely and relevant to the issues facing the VR program being addressed in the council's agenda. Usually it is more effective when data are accompanied with contextual explanations of how the information relates to the concerns being addressed by the VR agency and the SRC at that time.

This section discusses some types of data and reports that SRCs primarily use to review, analyze, and advise the VR agency about trends and issues that impact the effectiveness of service delivery and, ultimately, employment outcomes.

Common Performance Measures

The Workforce Innovation and Opportunity Act (WIOA) has established a set of national Common Performance Measures (CPM) that apply to VR agencies and identify minimum quality and quantity performance expectations. WIOA replaced the previous standards and indicators with Common Performance Measures. Prior to WIOA, there were set levels for each standard and indicator that applied to all VR agencies. Under WIOA, each VR agency has negotiated levels of performance that are determined for each measure (excluding Effectiveness in Serving Employers) with the Secretary of Education.

The measures are:

Employment 2nd quarter after exit-

> Percentage of program participants who are in unsubsidized employment during the second quarter after exiting from the program.

Employment 4th quarter after exit-

> Percentage of program participants who are in unsubsidized employment during the fourth quarter after exiting from the program.

Median earnings 2nd quarter after exit-

> Median earnings of program participants who are in unsubsidized employment during the second quarter after exit from the program.

Credential attainment rate-

> Percentage of program participants who obtain a recognized postsecondary credential, or a secondary school diploma or its recognized equivalent during participation in or within 1 year after exit from the program. A secondary school diploma or its recognized equivalent is only counted if the participant is employed or enrolled in a training program leading to a recognized postsecondary credential within 1 year after exit from the program.

Measurable skills gain rate –

> Percentage of program participants who, during a program year, are in an education or training program that leads to a recognized postsecondary credential or employment and who are achieving measurable skill gains toward such a credential or employment. There are five types of measurable skills gains:

1. Documented achievement of at least one educational functioning level of a participant who is receiving instruction below the postsecondary education level;
2. Documented attainment of a secondary school diploma or its recognized equivalent;
3. Secondary or postsecondary transcript or report card for a sufficient number of credit hours that shows a participant is meeting the DRS' academic standards (e.g., 15 hours of college credit with a GPA at or above the DRS requirement);
4. Satisfactory or better progress report, towards established milestones, such as completion of OJT or completion of one year of an apprenticeship program or similar milestones, from an employer or training provider who is providing training; or
5. Successful passage of an exam that is required for a particular occupation or progress in attaining technical or occupational skills as evidenced by trade-related benchmarks, such as knowledge-based exams.

Only participants are included in the performance calculations. Under WIOA, a vocational rehabilitation (VR) consumer becomes a participant after they have an IPE and have begun receiving services under the IPE.

Effectiveness in serving employers-

This measure is shared across all WIOA core programs. The state must select two of the following three measures:

1. Retention
   o The percentage of participants who exit and are employed with the same employer in the 2nd and 4th quarters after exit
2. Employer penetration rate
   o The percentage of employers using services from any of the WIOA core programs out of all employers in the state
3. Repeat business customer rate
   o The percentage of employers who receive services from WIOA core programs more than once during a three-year period.

The performance of a state VR agency in meeting performance measures is reported annually and integrated into the Unified or Combined State Plan. When a state agency does not meet required levels of performance, a program improvement plan must be developed jointly with RSA to meet the Common Performance Measures to assist the agency to meet the performance indicators.

Meeting or not meeting the Common Performance Measures may impact funding. It is therefore critical for the SRC and VR agency to jointly review performance measures to ensure that the VR agency is effectively meeting them and providing quality VR services to individuals with disabilities. If minimal standards are not being met, the obstacles preventing the agency from meeting standards need to be identified, and proactive strategies to improve performance need to be identified and implemented.

Budget and Expenditure Information

To evaluate whether the VR agency is administering funds efficiently and to evaluate the adequacy of resources, the SRC and the VR agency administration should regularly review fiscal information. This information includes expenditures for personnel services, administrative costs, consumer services, mandated levels of funding for pre-employment transition services and other costs of operating the VR program. This information can be found in the RSA-2 financial report submitted by state agencies to RSA. Funding changes resulting from state budget cuts or maintenance of effort penalties may require evaluation of the need to adjust current or future staffing or services.

Understanding the budget process of the state agency, including levels of spending authority, expenditure schedules, and appropriation requests is helpful and beneficial for the SRC. The VR agency *should* share fiscal information with the SRC when preparing budget proposals. This is especially important when budget cuts are under consideration. Likewise, information about increases in funding as a result of any federal reallotment will assist the SRC in understanding the level of resources available to the agency. Reallotment, the redistribution of funds turned back by other state agencies, has state match requirements.

The support of the SRC can be particularly critical if it becomes necessary for the VR agency to implement an OOS or make cuts in staffing or cost of services. By regularly sharing financial information and involving the SRC in fiscal decisions, the VR agency demonstrates both transparency in the utilization of its funding and the solicitation of input from its primary stakeholder.

Although each state differs in resources and data systems available. It is important that each SRC meet with the leadership of the agency and determine what data and reports are available and what the SRC needs in order to provide good guidance.

Policy Information

The reasoning for policy development can come from many directions. Inconsistent interpretations of existing written policy may be revealed through the quality assurance process. Budget constraints may require changes to service provision, requiring policy changes; changes in federal or state legislation and regulations can require policy amendments. Regardless of the source, the VR agency needs to establish a mechanism for routinely sharing new or revised policies and assessing the potential impact of policy changes on employment outcomes. Input from the SRC can also be beneficial in assessing the need to conduct a public meeting regarding policy change.

New council members often comment on how complicated the rules and policies for VR seem to be. Council members need not become experts on VR law and regulations, but it is reasonable to expect that members will learn applicable regulatory requirements when evaluating policy or proposing changes. When implementing responsibilities related to policy compliance, council members should be educated about what laws and regulations come into play and the priority of laws and policies. Of course, the U.S. Constitution is the "supreme law of the land," and all federal and state laws, including the Rehabilitation Act, must follow constitutional mandates. Federal laws have priority over state laws under the "supremacy clause" of the Constitution. Federal regulations are next in the hierarchy, followed by federal policy. The state constitution, state laws, state regulations, and state policy would follow in order. When in conflict, the policy, regulation, or law higher up on the hierarchy would prevail.

State VR policy must comply with the Rehabilitation Act, Title IV of the Workforce Innovation and Opportunity Act. The Act is implemented through federal regulation 34 CFR §361. RSA offering guidance and feedback to VR through agency monitoring reviews.

After federal law and regulation, state policies come into play. A state can implement policies that are not in conflict with the Act. A state can also require the VR agency to follow state policies where the Act allows state preferences or is silent on how to proceed. For example, many state agencies have a policy that requires an eligible individual seeking college education to attend an in-state college, if the course of study is available at that college. This is primarily a fiscal management strategy to favor lower, in-state tuition expenses over higher, out-of-state costs. Federal regulations allow fee schedule provisions that do not unduly restrict individuals' right to informed choice. Some of the states with in-state college mandates balance choice rights by allowing students to select higher-priced out-of-state colleges by paying the difference in cost. Other states do not have such restriction on the choice of college education. Both approaches are consistent with federal regulation.

Many states negotiate bulk contracts and have purchasing laws that require all state agencies to buy from a particular vendor, or, for example, purchase a particular brand of computer equipment. Such policies, if applied to VR clients' individualized plan for employment services and goods, can unreasonably restrict informed choice. If an SRC believes that state policy is causing a VR agency policy or practice to be out of compliance, it could bring the issue to the attention of the state VR agency administrator and, if appropriate, support agency efforts to bring the policy into compliance.

The definitive source for VR policy is the Rehabilitation Act and the federal regulations found in the Code of Federal Regulations (CFR). Other resources are as follows:

- *VR agency staff.* Most VR agencies have staff dedicated to policy analysis who can explain not only what the policy is but the origin of the policy.
- *The SRC.* SRC membership includes a representative from the Client Assistance Program, which has a policy consultation role in state plan development.
- *The website of the National Coalition of State Rehabilitation Councils* (www.ncsrc.net). This site provides links to policy resources as well as a listserv that council chairs can use to consult with other state council chairs.

Even if all the policies of a VR agency comply with the Rehabilitation Act, there may be some policies that could be improved. The SRC can play a very useful role by providing feedback on the clarity and readability of state VR policy. The VR policy provides direction for VR staff and can also serve to explain to VR consumers and the public what VR can do and under what circumstances it can do it. Policies that are understandable to the public can reduce a great deal of mistrust.

Management Information

VR agency management regularly collects and analyzes information as part of quality assurance measures and the assessment of service delivery, fiscal, and human resource needs. Typical reports generated by the VR agency include the following information:

1. Timeliness of case movement
2. Demographic data on individual disabilities
3. Caseload size
4. Information about individual program participants, such as transition youth or veterans
5. Participation and outcomes for minorities
6. Outcomes by each region or district in the state or territory
7. Outcomes and earnings for specific disability populations

While reports of this nature provide a snapshot for the VR agency, comparisons of data over time will indicate trends, both positive and problematic. Access to this information is important to enable SRCs to stay informed about the effectiveness and efficiency of the VR agency's operations.

Order of Selection

Another area where the SRC-VR partnership is critical is in determining when the state agency must develop and implement an OOS. Federal regulations provide that when states cannot provide the full range of services to all eligible individuals who apply due to lack of adequate resources, an order must be established indicating which eligible individuals will be served first (34 CFR §361.36). The regulations are very clear that individuals with the most significant disabilities receive first priority. In their partnership, VR consults with the SRC about five main areas relating to OOS: the need to establish an OOS; priority categories; criteria for determining individuals with the most significant disabilities; and implementation and administration of an OOS.

The *need to establish an OOS* is determined as the VR agency and the SRC review the financial status and resources of the organization. The review includes examination of how funds are expended for the provision of VR services using reports or other documents generated by the fiscal division of the agency, federal reports such as RSA-2 and RSA-113, and caseload flow reports. The participation of individuals in cost of services based on financial need and the agency fee schedule are also considered by the VR agency and the SRC when determining whether agencies should initiate an OOS. While VR is responsible for administering funds available through the VR basic, supported employment, and other grant funds, consideration of how those funds are used within the confines of the Rehabilitation Act as amended and federal regulations is an area where the SRC can have significant input.

Refining *priority categories* of the OOS by the VR agency in consultation with the SRC has major impact on who can be served and potentially when. States are obligated to closely consider the categories within OOS, ensuring that individuals with the most significant disabilities are served first. The SRC has a unique role to play here, especially when considering that some members of the SRC have received or are receiving VR services. These individuals have personal experience with the VR system and are sometimes best equipped to provide input regarding how to define or further refine categories that will determine who gets served and who has to wait until resources are available.

When establishing *criteria for determining individuals with the most significant disabilities (34 CFR 361.(5)(30),* the SRC and VR are guided by federal regulations that define what it means to be an "individual with a significant disability." The definition has three components: (1) the individual must have a severe physical or mental impairment that seriously limits one or more functional capacities in terms of an employment outcome; (2) the individual must be expected to require multiple VR services over an extended period of time; and (3) the individual has one or more physical or mental disabilities based on an assessment for determining eligibility and vocational needs to cause comparable substantial functional limitation.

WIOA made changes to order of selection by allowing VR agencies the opportunity to serve individuals who are employed (job-retention cases), regardless of the order in which they are assigned. WIOA provided new flexibility for VR agencies to help individuals retain their jobs, including individuals with less significant disabilities who might not normally be prioritized for services. Under WIOA, when a VR agency is under an order of selection— that is, must prioritize services to certain individuals because the agency lacks the resources to serve all eligible individuals— it may elect to assist individuals who need specific services or equipment to retain employment, even if these individuals would not otherwise receive services under the state's order of selection.

In terms of *implementation,* VR agencies must determine, and report to RSA, whether to establish and implement an OOS. States must reevaluate this determination whenever circumstances occur, such as a decrease in fiscal or personnel resources or an increase in program costs, and the states find that they cannot provide a full range of services for all eligible individuals. States must advise individuals on when they are determined eligible, what category they are placed in, and which categories are receiving services; individuals placed on a waiting list must be provided referral information to other available services and programs, in the event they seek services from other sources. Additionally, individuals must be advised of their rights to appeal their category assignment. Other activities include revising or updating state plans to reflect the OOS.

The *administration* of the OOS includes states' continuing to serve individuals currently receiving services, providing assessments to all individuals applying for services, and establishing and maintaining a waiting list for individuals who are eligible but do not meet the criteria for the categories being served at a given time. The SRC can assist VR in planning how to continue to provide services to individuals currently receiving services when an OOS is implemented. State agencies have some room to be creative and flexible when implementing OOS. The SRC-VR partnership is particularly valuable in finding ways to serve the maximum number of people with limited personnel and financial resources.

Unified or Combined State Plan

Under WIOA, states must submit a Unified (includes all six WIOA core programs) or Combined (contains all six WIOA core programs in addition to other eligible programs) State Plan. The State Plan is created for a four-year period and is updated and/or revised after the second year. The VR agency is jointly responsible for the Unified or Combined sections, in addition to the VR section of the State Plan.

A key document in the implementation of the public VR program, the state plan describes the policies and procedures adopted by a VR agency to administer the public VR program. The VR agency provides assurances that it will follow all of the requirements detailed in the Rehabilitation Act as it provides VR services to people with disabilities in that jurisdiction. The state plan describes how key components and processes of the Rehabilitation Act will be implemented and administered and, ultimately, how individuals with disabilities will be provided VR services leading to employment.

State Plan assurances provide that the SRC gets the information necessary to evaluate VR agency performance; that the VR agency receives the advice and recommendations of the SRC in establishing goals and developing policies to implement those goals; and that the SRC evaluates VR agency performance in achieving those goals. For example, the VR agency is required to provide the SRC with the same reports and information that the VR agency provides to RSA. By ensuring that they have access to information about VR agency performance, the Rehabilitation Act empowers the SRC to provide advice and recommendations from a position of being an informed collaborator.

Specifically, Section 105 of the Act requires the SRC to assist in the preparation of the State Plan and amendments to the plan. The State Plan contains various sections, one of which relates directly to the input of the SRC. This section is a summary of input and recommendations of the SRC and the response of VR, including explanations for rejection of input or recommendations. (See example in Appendix E)

Comprehensive System of Personnel Development

The Comprehensive System of Personnel Development (CSPD) section of the Vocational Rehabilitation portion of the Unified or Combined State Plan (SP) offers a detailed look at staffing levels and the state VR agency plan for recruitment, preparation, and retention of qualified personnel.

The CSPD includes a description of the procedures and activities the State agency will undertake to ensure an adequate supply of qualified staff.

The State Unit must develop a system for determining on an annual basis-

- the number of personnel employed including ratios of qualified rehabilitation counselors to clients;
- projection of the number of personnel needed in five years based on projections of number of individuals to be served;
- the number of personnel who are expected to retire or leave;
- the number of institutions of higher education within the state that are preparing rehabilitation professionals;
- the number of students enrolled in such programs;
- the number of students who graduated with certification or licensure or credentials to qualify for certification or licensure;
- a system for continuing education;
- the establishment and maintenance of standards that are consistent with any national or state approved or recognized certification, licensing, registration, or other comparable requirements that apply to personnel providing vocational rehabilitation services;
- the establishment of education and experience requirements.

Since the quality of personnel and the training provided to those personnel can have a direct impact on the performance of the VR agency, the SRC has a role in reviewing the plan and offering feedback to the state VR agency.

Partnerships

Systemic issues involving partnerships may be less apparent in data and reports. Public comment, focus groups, and review of the VR agency's and other departments' policies or practices may be necessary to answer these questions:

- How are working relationships between departments impacting effectiveness?
- Do conflicting policies from different departments create barriers for consumers?
- Are the roles and responsibilities of VR and other agencies clear to the agencies as well as the consumers?

As a member of the SRC, the Client Assistance Program (CAP) representative can often provide input on systemic issues. Further, because the membership of the SRC includes representation from a number of disciplines, the SRC may be able to advise the VR agency on effective partnering with other agencies.

The SRC Role in the Comprehensive Statewide Needs Assessment

VR agencies and SRCs are jointly required in the Rehabilitation Act of 1973 to conduct a triennial Comprehensive Statewide Needs Assessment (CSNA) which describes the rehabilitation needs of individuals with disabilities residing within the state. The results of the CSNA are included in the Unified or Combined State Plan. The CSNA is the basis for the state plan goals, objectives, and strategies.

It must describe the rehabilitation needs of:

- Individuals with the most significant disabilities, including their need for supported employment services;
- Individuals with disabilities who are minorities;

- Individuals with disabilities who have been unserved or underserved by the vocational rehabilitation program;
- Individuals with disabilities served through other components of the statewide workforce development system;
- Youth with disabilities, and students with disabilities, including their need for pre-employment transition services or other transition services;
- An assessment of the needs of individuals with disabilities for transition services and pre-employment transition services, and the extent to which such services are coordinated with transition services provided under the Individuals with Disabilities Education Act in order to meet the needs of individuals with disabilities;
- An assessment of the need to establish, develop, or improve community rehabilitation programs within the State.

The SRC should be involved as a partner with VR in the following stages in the CSNA process:
- Planning the assessment goals.
- Collecting data and providing community links.
- Reviewing findings.
- Developing recommendations.
- Using the CSNA findings to Inform the VR section of the Unified or Combined state plan goals.

RSA's guide to meeting the requirements of a CSNA can be found on RSA's website at http://www2.ed.gov/programs/rsabvrs/resources.html#needs-assessment.

Periodically reviewing the results of the CSNA is a valuable activity in determining whether the goals and objectives established by the VR agency are responsive to the needs identified in the CSNA by consumers and stakeholders of the VR program. Comparing the CSNA with other management information can also provide both the SRC and VR direction in defining future actions.

Participation of the SRC with the State Agency in the Monitoring

Section 107 of the Rehabilitation Act of 1973, as amended, requires the commissioner of the RSA to conduct annual reviews and periodic on-site monitoring of programs authorized under Title I of the Rehabilitation Act to determine whether a state VR agency is complying substantially with the provisions of its State Plan under Section 101 of the Rehabilitation Act and with the evaluation standards and performance indicators established under Section 106.

RSA conducts the annual review by collecting and analyzing data and information related to performance and compliance of VR and independent living programs from multiple sources such as: State Plan amendments; standard and indicators reports; RSA-2; RSA-113; RSA-911 and other data reports. These reports are analyzed and feedback given to the state.

In addition, RSA conducts on-site monitoring of the state VR and independent living programs every three years. It engages in discussions on-site with the state agency staff, the SRC, the Statewide Independent Living Council, persons with disabilities who receive program services, and stakeholders. They also analyze data and reports related to performance and compliance of the VR and IL programs from multiple sources.

Following the review, the RSA team develops observations and recommendations for the VR agency to improve program performance.

The RSA monitoring team considers several SRC items:

- Onsite meeting(s) with SRC
- SRC annual report
- SRC State Plan and recommendations
- Input received at State Plan public hearings and other forums
- CSNA

(See example of SRC monitoring visit "guidebook" in Appendix E.)

Consumer Satisfaction Survey

Section 105(4) indicates:

> to the extent feasible, conduct a review and analysis of the effectiveness of, and consumer satisfaction with—
>
> **(A)** all the functions performed by the designated State Agency,
> **(B)** Vocational Rehabilitation Services provided by State Agencies and other private/public entities delivering services to persons with disabilities, and
> **(C)** employment outcomes achieved by persons receiving services under this Title.

In assessing consumer satisfaction, SRCs and state agencies employ a variety of methods and strategies. Some contract with public or private research companies or colleges and universities; others develop their own methods within the SRC itself. Regardless of approach, measuring satisfaction involves measuring attitudes, and from a research perspective, can be categorized as descriptive in nature. Such research typically employs written surveys or questionnaires, structured interviews, focus groups, or other similar activities.

Considering satisfaction with a state VR agency involves looking at consumers' satisfaction with VR service delivery and outcomes. VR services have several stages, including application, eligibility determination, in-services, employment, closure, and follow-up. To be most useful, the evaluation should address consumer satisfaction with each stage of service delivery. While it is easier to measure satisfaction at closure, due to the extended length of some VR plans, the consumer may not be able to accurately recall his or her initial experience at closure. For this reason, satisfaction surveys that include input from consumers at different points in their VR experience are probably most informative. Though it may not be feasible to survey every consumer of a VR agency, an adequate sample size should generate accurate and usable information. The sample size will vary according to the methodology used. Care should be taken to make the surveys accessible to all individuals participating in the program, considering language, disability, and level of education. Alternative formats and languages must be used. If the survey is not accessible to all consumers, the results will not accurately reflect overall satisfaction.

Questions asked in a survey generally include the consumer's experience in interacting with agency staff, including the VR counselor; the nature of the counseling relationship; input into the rehabilitation planning process; satisfaction with services received; and satisfaction with the ultimate outcome (work, salary, benefits, etc.). Surveys can be developed using different approaches, but one common method is to employ a Likert scale, which asks the consumer whether he or she strongly agrees (SA), agrees (A), is neutral (N), disagrees (D), or strongly disagrees (SD) with a statement. For example:

1. Information provided to me was easy to understand.   SA A N D SD
2. I actively participated in the development of my plan.   SA A N D SD

For examples of individual state consumer satisfaction surveys, contact individual SRCs directly for more information. Links can be found on the NCSRC website at www.ncsrc.net.

Regardless of their methodology, consumer satisfaction studies provide a wealth of information about state VR programs that can be used by VR to improve service delivery and to provide governmental entities and the general public with positive information about VR. The SRC's role is to recommend how to utilize the information gained.

Public Participation

Federal regulations pertaining to public participation requirements or public meetings are designed to ensure that states gather input from critical stakeholders when planning for and providing VR services. Additionally, as reviewed above, states are required to include a summary of input by the SRC in developing the State Plan. As a partner to VR agencies, SRCs have a significant role in conducting public meetings for the purpose of informing the State Plan and the VR services that are included in that Plan.

According to 34 CFR §361.20, states must conduct public meetings prior to adopting substantial policies and procedures governing the provision of VR services designated under the state plan. The purpose and most critical component of public meetings is to ensure that the public, in particular individuals with disabilities, have the opportunity to comment on the goods and services they receive through the VR agency. With partnership as a hallmark of the primary relationship between the individuals receiving services and the agency providing services, the partnering role of the SRC with VR in planning and implementing public meetings becomes even more important. The SRC-VR agency partnership creates opportunities for various stakeholders to make their desires, preferences, and experiences known. When SRCs collaborate with VR to schedule and conduct public meetings, attendance increases, representation of stakeholders is broader, and comments are deeper in depth and breadth; the collaboration provides a stronger forum for those who may not otherwise speak their minds regarding the VR program.

One challenge in many states is poor attendance at public meetings. To combat lack of participation, some states take advantage of the SRC-VR partnership to conduct public meetings in conjunction with statewide training activities where individuals with disabilities, their families, and service providers are gathered. In several states, public meetings are held during advocacy group state meetings or conventions where larger groups of individuals come together.

Although states have great flexibility in the way public meetings are organized, certain guidelines must be followed. The public must be provided with appropriate and sufficient notice of the meetings throughout the state in accordance with state law governing public meetings. When no state law exists regarding the conduct of public meetings, the VR agency must consult with the SRC regarding procedures to be used in administering public meetings.

For primary stakeholders to be able to fully participate in public meetings, the state must ensure that appropriate modes of communication are used when providing notice of public meetings and providing materials that will be used prior to or during the meetings. The SRC and VR must collaborate to ensure that all forums, hearings, and meetings are fully accessible to individuals with disabilities. Accessibility includes physical access to buildings, meeting rooms, restroom facilities, and parking. It also includes access to printed materials, which must be provided in formats such as Braille, large print, and electronic files for individuals who cannot access standard print. Interpreters, computer assisted real time (CART), and assistive listening devices must be provided for individuals who cannot hear or understand speech. Partnering with

VR agencies to ensure those individuals with disabilities have access to public meetings and VR services is another area where SRC members serve in the obvious capacity of consumer voice.

Partnering between VR and the SRC to meet the federal requirement for public participation demonstrates in real time what the spirit of the law intends. When constituents see and experience that the state VR agency and the largely consumer driven SRC cooperate to make sure the public has the opportunity to have input, this is a win-win for everyone. VR has the valued-added input from individuals with disabilities and other primary stakeholders, and those same stakeholders have a voice in the way VR services are developed and provided.

Selection and Evaluation of Impartial Hearing Officers

Individuals applying for and receiving VR services have a basic right to request a review of determinations made by the state VR agency. States are required to develop and implement policies and procedures to ensure that individuals who are dissatisfied with services may request a timely review of decisions made by the VR agency, through either an impartial due process hearing or a voluntary mediation process. In general, before escalating to a higher level review, it is best practice to attempt to resolve consumer concerns early between the individual and the VR counselor or through the state's informal dispute resolution process.

The impartial due process hearing is conducted by an impartial hearing officer. According to 7(16) and 361.5(24) of the implementing Regulations such officers may not be employees of a public agency, other than an administrative law judge, hearing examiner, or employee of an institution of higher education. In addition, the impartial hearing officer may not be a member of the SRC or an existing or former consumer of services. He/she should be knowledgeable about the VR program and applicable federal and state laws, regulations, and policies governing the provision of VR services. He/she shall have been trained in respect to the performance of official duties and shall have no personal, professional, or financial interest that could affect the objectivity of the individual.

Federal regulations do not require that the SRC and the VR agency jointly identify qualified and impartial hearing officers. Rather, the state maintains a list of qualified and impartial hearing officers in accordance with procedures established in the state. The essential role of the SRC is to assist the VR agency in identifying qualified hearing officers who have an understanding of or the ability to understand the nature of the Rehabilitation Act as amended, state and federal regulations pertaining to the provision of VR services, and the policies and procedures developed and maintained by the state. In some states, SRC members help VR develop the criteria for hiring qualified hearing officers and participate in interviews. Additionally, they may partner to develop and conduct training for hearing officers.

Advocacy

The SRC advocates with federal and state legislators to promote the public VR program as a sound investment that leads to the employment of individuals with significant disabilities.

In general, federal funds may not be used to engage in lobbying activities (Lobbying Disclosure Act of 1995, P.L. 104-65). Unless otherwise prohibited by state law, nonfederal funds can be used in lobbying activities (Michaels, 1998). Lobbying may include the following activities:

- Attempts to influence the outcome of any federal, state, or local election, referendum, initiative, or similar procedure

- Attempts to influence the introduction, enactment, or modification of federal or state legislation by efforts to utilize state or local officials to engage in similar activities
- Attempts to influence the introduction, enactment, or modification of federal or state legislation by trying to gain the support of part or all of the general public (Michaels, 1998).

Thus, an important distinction needs to be made between lobbying and advocacy. While lobbying can be a subset of advocacy, it is narrower in scope with the specific focus of convincing legislators to vote in a requested manner on a particular legislative proposal (Michaels, 1998). SRC members should make sure that no federal funds are used to support lobbying activities. Of course, SRC members as private citizens, not representing or acting on behalf of the SRC, can lobby with their own funds while exercising their first amendment right of free speech.

SRC members, unlike VR agency employees, can take a more credible stance than VR employees when advocating for the VR program. Stated differently, unlike employees, they are not likely to be told by legislative or other decision makers that they are merely attempting to save their own jobs. Also, SRC members who were past VR clients or their family members can demonstrate the effectiveness of VR programs when advocating for individuals with disabilities. However, the SRC should fully understand the importance of specific state laws and regulations concerning advocacy activities with state legislators.

Summary

This chapter has presented an overview of the mandated activities that SRCs must perform in their active partnership with the state VR agency and has described how such activities might be carried out. As indicated, a fully functioning SRC is deeply involved in the review of, and input into, most of the core responsibilities of a state-federal VR program. As each state is organized and functions somewhat differently, it should be noted that there is no "one way" a task might be accomplished. SRC members are strongly recommended to use documents such as this one, as well as input from colleagues locally, regionally, and nationally, to determine how to shape their work.

References

Code of Federal Regulations. Part 361—State Vocational Rehabilitation Services Program. Title34, Parts 300 to 399, Revised as of July 1, 2017.

Lobbying Disclosure Act of 1995, Pub. L. No. 104-65 (1995).

Rehabilitation Services Administration. (2010). *RSA fiscal year 2010 monitoring: State vocational rehabilitation and independent living programs information guide.* Washington, DC: U.S. Department of Education, Office of Special Education and Rehabilitative Services, Rehabilitation Services Administration. Retrieved from http://www2.ed.gov/rschstat/eval/rehab/107-reports/2010/monitoring-info-guide.pdf

Workforce Investment Act of 1998, Pub. L. No. 105–220, 112 Stat. 936 (1998).

Chapter 5:
SRC Resources

To be a full and effective partner with the state vocational rehabilitation (VR) agency, it is critical for State Rehabilitation Councils (SRCs) to have a full understanding of the scope of their resources for information and support. Resources come in all shapes and sizes. They can come in the form of reference materials, data, reports, and laws and regulations. Resources also come in the form of content experts, training entities, and staff support, as well as partner and stakeholder relationships. It is important for SRCs to be fully aware of and have access to resources, rather than depending on the state agency to define and provide them. This chapter outlines several major resources. The resources are discussed in terms of their relevance and frequency of use for SRC members.

Rehabilitation Act of 1973, as Amended

The Rehabilitation Act of 1973, as amended, is the authorizing federal legislation on which the VR program and the SRC are based. It is important for SRC members to have access to this document as a reference, to review both agency and council purpose and duties, and to gain a fuller context by accessing other aspects of the law. The Act in its entirety can be accessed at https://www2.ed.gov/policy/speced/leg/rehab/ rehabilitation-act-of-1973-amended-by-wioa.pdf, The VR program is detailed in Title IV of the Workforce Innovation and Opportunities Act (WIOA). See Appendix C for sections of the Act that pertain to the State Rehabilitation Council (SRC).

Rehabilitation Services Administration

The Rehabilitation Services Administration (RSA), under the U.S. Department of Education, Office of Special Education and Rehabilitation Services, is the federal agency that administers and supports the state VR program, including the SRC. RSA also administers a number of related programs that are useful to individuals with disabilities and support VR efforts, including the Client Assistance Program (CAP). CAP reports should be of interest to SRCs, given the direct relationship and CAP's required membership and participation on SRCs.

The RSA website—**http://rsa.ed.gov/**—offers information on all of its programs and projects, and provides extensive information on the Workforce Innovation and Opportunity Act (WIOA). The website provides links to rehabilitation legislation and regulations, as well as RSA issuances such as policy directives and information memoranda. The guidance is arranged by program on the website.

RSA designates a NCSRC liaison who is available as a resource to SRCs and who participates in NCSRC conference calls, at national meetings, and by telephone or email.

VR Federal Regulations

The VR federal regulations, 34 CFR §361—located at https://www.govinfo.gov/ content/ pkg/CFR-2017-title34-vol2/xml/CFR-2017-title34-vol2- part361.xml—are the main resource for understanding SRC duties and requirements, as well as the full scope of the VR program and its basic rules and requirements. The web link breaks down the regulations by chapter for ease of navigation. Having knowledge of and easy access to this reference is a necessity for SRCs, in terms of being able to review, analyze, and advise the state agency in the performance of its duties. Many state VR agency policies are based on these regulations, and VR state agency policies cannot contradict the federal regulations.

State VR Agency Websites

Individual state agency websites vary considerably in terms of content and organization. Most offer basic program and contact information. Several state agencies post information that is extremely relevant to SRCs, including annual performance reports, the current state plan for VR, and agency policy manuals. Most state websites can be accessed by Googling "vocational rehabilitation" with the state name.

National Coalition of State Rehabilitation Councils

The website of the National Coalition of State Rehabilitation Councils (NCSRC)—at **http://www.ncsrc.net/**—offers opportunities for SRCs to become more informed on their roles and makes available numerous tools, including a national listserv for members. This is the only national link that exists between state SRCs. The ability to discuss issues and concerns across states helps all SRCs be more fully informed on the VR system. The National Coalition of State Rehabilitation Councils is an optional membership organization. Several resources are available to nonmembers as well as members. The coalition meets regularly by conference call and also schedules face-to-face meetings in conjunction with annual spring and fall conferences held by the Council of State Administrators of Vocational Rehabilitation (CSAVR).

Links to individual member SRCs can be found at ncsrc.net- click on "Membership".

Client Assistance Program

It is important for SRC members to understand the role of their state's CAP. CAPs are funded through grants from RSA. Every SRC is required to have a member from CAP, and this person does not have membership term limits. The purpose of CAP is to advise and inform clients, client applicants, and other individuals with disabilities of available services and benefits under the Rehabilitation Act of 1973, as amended, and under Title I of the Americans with Disabilities Act (ADA). In addition, CAP may assist and advocate for clients and client applicants in relation to projects, programs, and services provided under the Rehabilitation Act.

CAPs can provide legal representation to individuals involved in formal appeal hearings with VR agencies. CAPs write an annual report for RSA that provides demographic information regarding individuals served, as well as information on outreach and systemic advocacy efforts. These reports are an excellent source of information to SRCs for reviewing, analyzing, and advising VR programs. Information on CAPs is available on the RSA website at https://rsa.ed.gov/programs.cfm?pc=CAP, with a link available to regulations under the "Laws,

Regulations, Guidance, and other communication" heading. Local CAPs can be found through the National Disability Rights Network website at https://www.ndrn.org/about/ndrn-member-agencies/.

Parent Training and Information Centers

Funded through the U.S. Department of Education under the Individuals with Disabilities Education Act, parent training and information centers (PTIs) provide training and assistance to the families of children (birth to 26) with all types of disabilities. Every state has one or more parent centers. Most staff and board members are parents of children with disabilities. A PTI representative is a required SRC member. More information on this program is available at https://www2.ed.gov/programs/oseppic/index.html. To find local PTIs, visit https://www.parentcenterhub.org/find-your-center.

Statewide Independent Living Council and Centers for Independent Living

A representative from the Statewide Independent Living Council (SILC) is a required member of the SRC. The SILC and the SRC are to partner and collaborate on issues of common concern. To most effectively work with the SILC, SRCs need to have a clear understanding of the SILC's purpose, as well as the purpose of centers for independent living (CILs) and the differences of the two councils. Among other responsibilities, the SILC collaborates with the VR agency to develop the state plan for independent living. Contact information for all SILCs and CILs nationwide can be found at https://www.ilru.org/projects/silc-net/silc-directory.

Communication Tools

Many SRCs refer to, or have adopted, formal rules of order such as Robert's Rules of Order. Members' familiarity with the rules varies, as does each SRC's adherence to the rules. It may be helpful for SRCs to educate members on rules of order or provide easy references to help with meeting functioning. Information on Robert's Rules, including a quick reference, can be found on http://www.rulesonline.com/. Information is also provided in Appendix D.

SRCs may also want to offer members tips or guidelines regarding e-mail and conference call etiquette. These kinds of supports can help make council communication and meetings run smoothly and can also help with relationship building. A number of online resources can be located with a quick web search, and SRCs can use and modify what works best for their individual council.

Council of State Administrators of Vocational Rehabilitation

The Council of State Administrators of Vocational Rehabilitation (CSAVR) is composed of the chief administrators of the 80 public VR agencies serving eligible individuals with disabilities in states, the District of Columbia, and the territories. Their mission is to maintain and enhance a strong, effective, and efficient national program of public VR services which empowers individuals with disabilities to achieve employment, economic self-sufficiency, independence, and inclusion and integration into our communities. CSAVR created the National Employment Team (the NET), a national network of the 80 public VR programs that supports a united or "one-company" approach to working with business customers. The NET's vision is "to create a coordinated approach to serving business customers through a national VR team that specializes in employer development, business consulting, and corporate relations." The NET supports a dual customer base, meeting the employment needs of business through the qualified applicants and support services provided by the public VR system. VR consumers receive better career planning and employment supports when VR works with business customers to better understand their needs and expectations.

It is important for SRC members to understand the relationship between their state's VR program and CSAVR. CSAVR provides leadership and insight on national trends and issues with the VR program. Also, SRC members are sometimes asked by their VR agency to represent their state and attend CSAVR conferences.

The National Council of State Rehabilitation Councils schedules its face-to-face meetings and trainings to coincide with the national CSAVR spring and fall conferences.

More information on CSAVR and its initiatives and positions is available at https://www.csavr.org/.

National Council of State Agencies for the Blind

The National Council of State Agencies for the Blind (NCSAB) is an organization comprising the administrators of state agencies and/or service delivery units within the larger state public VR programs responsible for the delivery of specialized services that enable individuals who are blind or visually impaired to achieve personal and vocational independence. This council provides a specialized forum for administrators of member agencies to study, deliberate, and act upon matters affecting rehabilitation and other services for individuals who are blind or visually impaired. In addition, it is a resource for the formulation and expression of the collective points of view of member agencies on all issues affecting provision of services. Finally, the organization also serves as an advisory body to and establishes and maintains liaison with RSA and all other federal agencies as they develop policies and administer programs affecting services for individuals who are blind or visually impaired.

More information about NCSAB and its initiatives and positions is available at **http://www.ncsab.org/**. SRC members who are responsible for reviewing, analyzing, and advising VR programs and services for the blind and visually impaired should be informed about this organization. Not all SRCs have this responsibility. If the state has a separate agency for the blind, there may be a separately designated SRC or independent commission to attend to the matters regarding this separate agency.

Consortia of Administrators for Native American Rehabilitation

The Consortia of Administrators for Native American Rehabilitation (CANAR) is an organization comprising administrators of Native American rehabilitation programs. The purpose of the consortia is to study, deliberate, and act upon matters affecting rehabilitation, with the ultimate goal of expanding quality rehabilitation services to Native American persons with disabilities. CANAR serves as a resource for the formulation and expression of collective points of view of administrators for Native American rehabilitation on issues affecting rehabilitation on reservations, trust territories, Alaskan Native villages, and across the country and to disseminate these views to service providers, related facilities, companies, and concerned citizens. In addition, the consortia provides a means of communication with related organizations and governmental bodies on matters related to rehabilitation service provision, education, and research. SRCs from states with Native American VR programs should be informed on where to find information on the consortia's initiatives and positions: http://canar.us/.

National Clearinghouse for Rehabilitation Training Materials

The National Clearinghouse for Rehabilitation Training Materials (https://ncrtm.ed.gov/) is sponsored by RSA. The clearinghouse serves the VR profession as a centralized resource for the development, collection, dissemination, and utilization of training materials; as a forum for advancing knowledge through applied research and open dialogue; and as a marketplace for career and staff development.

The mission of the clearinghouse is to advocate for the advancement of best practices in rehabilitation counseling through the development, collection, dissemination, and utilization of professional information, knowledge, and skill. Initiatives that may be developed under this rubric include (a) training material publication and archive; (b) technical assistance in training development; (c) distance-based continuing education; (d) professional recruitment/employment services; (e) professional networking and forums; (f) applied research and data warehousing; and (g) special events and projects.

Resources for Consumer Satisfaction Surveys

The SRC has a primary role in collaborating with the state VR agency on the consumer satisfaction survey design, as well as the analysis of survey results. A database of several different state consumer satisfaction surveys can be found at http://vocational-rehab.com/resources/customer-satisfaction-survey/. This information can be a helpful resource to SRC members as they review, analyze, and advise on this topic.

National Rehabilitation Association

The National Rehabilitation Association (NRA) is a membership organization for professionals involved in the VR field. This association provides up-to-date information on advocacy, issues, and networking opportunities. It often writes about its positions on specific issues and posts them on its website, and this information might help inform a council on a matter of interest. The National Rehabilitation Association website is located at **http://www.nationalrehab.org/**.

Councils on Developmental Disabilities

Councils on Developmental Disabilities were created through federal legislation to address the needs of individuals with developmental disabilities regarding self-determination, independence, and community integration. Such councils exist in every state and territory, and sometimes they collaborate with SRCs on issues of common concern. Individual state contact information can be found at https://nacdd.org/councils/.

Institute on Rehabilitation Issues

The Institute on Rehabilitation Issues (IRI) was a valuable resource for information relevant to all of the VR programs, as it published documents on an annual basis intended to address emerging VR topics and issues. Many of the publications remain very relevant to the VR programs today. The IRI was sponsored by RSA, CSAVR, and the TACE programs at the University of Arkansas, The George Washington University, and previously the University of Wisconsin–Stout. A full list of IRI publications is available for download at **https://ncrtm.ed.gov**. The direct link to an accessible format of the 36th IRI on the SRC-VR Partnership is https://ncrtm.ed.gov/Download.aspx?type=doc&id=4693.

Disability.gov

Disability.gov is a national website managed by the Office of Disability Employment Policy (ODEP) in partnership with 21 other federal agencies. It offers comprehensive disability-related resources on programs, services, laws, and regulations. Additionally, SRCs can search this database to obtain training resources to help enhance the functioning of SRCs. For instance, resources regarding disability etiquette, disability awareness, disability sensitivity, and person-first language can be found through this website using the search window. Many SRC members come to the SRC with specific content expertise, but they may need training and assistance with overall disability information. This website is located at http://www.disability.gov/.

U.S. Census Bureau: American FactFinder

The Census Bureau provides demographic information regarding specific communities within specific states, using American FactFinder: **http://factfinder.census.gov/home/saff/main.html?_lang=en**. This information addresses population, disability, and race/ethnicity, as well as other relevant data elements. SRC members should have insight into their state's and community's demographics. State and community information from the Census Bureau can help identify unserved and underserved populations.

Disability and Business Technical Assistance Center

The National Institute on Disability and Rehabilitation Research (NIDRR) funds 10 regional ADA National Network Centers to provide training, guidance, and information on the ADA to their respective regional areas. The website, http://www.adata.org/, helps users locate their region's Disability and Business Technical Assistance Center (DBTAC). These centers are excellent resources to help SRCs and VR agencies understand the ADA and how it applies to their mission and goals.

U.S. Government Accountability Office

The Government Accountability Office (GAO) is an independent nonpartisan agency that works for Congress and investigates how the federal government spends taxpayer dollars. The GAO audits various federally funded agencies' operations for efficiency and effectiveness and reports on how well government programs and policies are meeting their goals and objectives. Because the VR program is federally funded, the GAO has written reports regarding the VR program and will write related reports in the future as the program evolves. The GAO also might research and report on related federally funded programs that could be relevant to the VR agency; an example would be Social Security. GAO reports might be of significant interest to the SRC, and SRC members might even be contacted as part of a GAO study. The most effective way to be in touch with the GAO on VR issues is to browse its website at **http://www.gao.gov/** by topic or agency or subscribe to its e-mail list and tailor the subscription to the topic or agency of interest.

Ticket to Work

Ticket to Work is an employment program through Social Security to assist eligible beneficiaries with disabilities in going to work. Ticket to Work offers employment networks to give beneficiaries options for assistance with return to work. Understanding how the Ticket to Work program relates to the VR program and other stakeholders (some of which might be employment networks) is helpful for SRC members.

The Ticket to Work website, https://yourtickettowork.ssa.gov/index.html, provides a variety of resources, including information on programs related to the Ticket to Work legislation, a directory listing each state's work incentives planning and assistance grants, and a description of the work incentives planning and assistance services. Social Security regulations about earned income and available work incentives and support services are critical pieces of information in VR and therefore can be very relevant to the work of SRCs.

Assistive Technology Act Programs

RSA provides grants to states for the provision of comprehensive statewide programs of information and support for assistive technology. Assistive Technology Act programs often work closely with VR programs as a source of information, training, and consumer programs related to assistive technology. The state Assistive Technology Act program can be a source of information and guidance for the SRC, as it is an expert on the topic of assistive technology. More information is available at https://www.ataporg.org/. Contact information for each state assistive technology project can be found at https://www.at3center.net/stateprogram.

O*NET

O*NET (see **http://www.onetcenter.org/**) is a nationwide resource and database for occupational information. It provides information such as job qualifications, education/training requirements, and employment outlook information for various careers. SRCs may find the information valuable as they review and advise on topics such as program development.

Job Accommodations Network

The Job Accommodations Network (see **http://askjan.org/**), a service provided through ODEP, is a comprehensive resource for information and guidance on workplace accommodations and disability employment issues. VR programs often use this resource, and SRCs need to be aware of this Network..

Office of Employment and Disability Policy

ODEP offers additional resources, programs, and information regarding the employment of individuals with disabilities; see **http://www.dol.gov/odep/**.

Protection and Advocacy Systems

Protection and Advocacy Systems (P&As)—congressionally-mandated, legally-based disability rights organizations—are located in every state. These programs sometimes are umbrella organizations that include CAP, but not in every state. Protection and Advocacy Programs may be active in disability rights issues that are important to the SRC. A directory available at https://acl.gov/programs/aging-and-disability-networks/state-protection-advocacy-systems provides the locations of these programs throughout the country.

National Institute on Disability and Rehabilitation Research

The National Institute on Disability and Rehabilitation Research (NIDRR), funded through the U.S. Department of Education Office of Special Education and Rehabilitation Services, offers comprehensive research information on topics of disability and rehabilitation.
- NIDRR conducts research on areas of interest to the VR field. NIDRR usually presents some of their more important research studies at the CSAVR conferences.

More information regarding NIDRR can be found at https://acl.gov/about-acl/about-national-institute-disability-independent-living-and-rehabilitation-research.

VR Needs Assessment Guide

The *Vocational Rehabilitation Needs Assessment Guide* (available at https://www2.ed.gov/programs/rsabvrs/needs-assessment-guide.html) and appendices from the U.S. Department of Education's RSA provide state VR agencies and SRCs with basic tools needed to meet the requirements of a fully developed comprehensive statewide needs assessment.

RSA Monitoring and Technical Assistance Guide

Section 107(a) of the Rehabilitation Act of 1973 (Act), as amended by title IV of the Workforce Innovation and Opportunity Act (WIOA), requires the Commissioner of the Rehabilitation Services Administration (RSA) to conduct annual reviews and periodic on-site monitoring of programs authorized under title I of the Act, in order to determine whether a vocational rehabilitation (VR) agency is complying substantially with the provisions of its State Plan, and evaluation standards and performance indicators. To fulfill, in part, this requirement, RSA has developed the Monitoring and Technical Assistance Guide through which it will provide technical assistance to, and review the progress of, VR agencies toward compliance with requirements under the Act, and assess improvements in the performance of the VR program and compliance with pertinent Federal programmatic and fiscal requirements. This Guide can be found at https://www2.ed.gov/rschstat/eval/rehab/107-reports/index.html.

Annual Disability Statistics Compendium

The *Disability Statistics Compendium* is an annual publication of statistics on people with disabilities and government programs that serve the population with disabilities. It is modeled after the *Statistical Abstracts of the United States,* published yearly by the U.S. Department of Commerce. The compendium is designed to serve as a reference guide to government publications. At the bottom of each table, the source of data appearing in each table is presented. These referenced sources contain additional statistics and information about the way the data were collected and the statistics were generated. The compendium can be downloaded at **www.DisabilityCompendium.org**.

Conclusion

While this chapter has not included every available resource, it can serve as a reference tool for SRCs so they can better understand the full scope of resources available to the council, the VR program, and individuals with disabilities. Each SRC will define its resources according to what is most relevant to its state and program. These resources can be used as a starting point for orientation and training of SRC members and can also be used to locate valuable tools to assist the SRC in carrying out its mandated duties.

Appendix A:
Major RSA Policy Guidance Documents Related to the VR Program

RSA Guidance Documents that may be of interest to SRCs are listed below. The full text of each is available at **http://rsa.ed.gov.** Go to "Legislation and Policy," then to "Sub-regulatory guidance". then to "All sub-regulatory guidance by date issued".

Note that other Guidance Documents are available at the RSA website. Those listed in this Appendix are limited to those thought to be most applicable to SRC interests.

RSA Technical Assistance Circulars (TAC):

The TAC giving guidance to SRCs (TAC 12-01) was retired and has not yet been reissued..

- **Guidance for Validating Jointly Required Performance Data Submitted under the Workforce Innovation and Opportunity Act (WIOA)** TAC-19-01 (December 19, 2018)
- **Performance Accountability Guidance for Workforce Innovation and Opportunity Act Title I, Title II, Title III and Title IV Core Programs** TAC-17-01 (August 17, 2017)
- **WIOA Annual Performance Report Submission** TAC-17-05 (Sept. 11, 2017)
- **Vision for the State Vocational Rehabilitation Services Program as a Partner in the Workforce Development System under the Workforce Innovation and Opportunity Act** TAC-15-02 (August 17, 2015)
- **Vision for the One-Stop Delivery System under the Workforce Innovation and Opportunity Act (WIOA)** TAC-15-01 (August 13,2015)
- **Reorganization of the Designated State Agency and the Designated State Unit for the Vocational Rehabilitation Program** TAC-13-02 (July 9, 2013)
- **Provision of Vocational Rehabilitation Services to an Individual by More Than One Agency** TAC-12-04 (June 11, 2012)
- **Organizational Structure and Non-Delegable Responsibilities of the Designated State Unit for the Vocational Rehabilitation Program.** TAC-12-03 (April 16, 2012)
  - **Self-employment, Telecommuting, and Establishing a Small Business as**

RSA Policy Directives (PD):

- **Revised Case Service Report (RSA-911) for implementation** beginning in Program Year (PY) 2020, beginning July 1, 2020. PD-19-03
- **Retirement of Certain Policy Issuances** PD-17-01 (January 18, 2017)
- **Workforce and Innovation and Opportunity Act (WIOA) Requirements for Unified and Combined State Plans** PD-16-03 (March 9, 2016)
- **Implementation of Informed Choice** PD-01-03 (January 17, 2001) Appendix B: Frequently Used Acronyms

Appendix B:
Frequently Used Acronyms

121 programs: Native American vocational rehabilitation
504: Section 504 of the Rehabilitation Act, which protects various civil rights of people with
    disabilities
AA: Alcoholics Anonymous
ACB: American Council for the Blind
ADA: Americans with Disabilities Act
ADD: Attention Deficit Disorder
ADHD: Attention deficit with hyperactivity disorder
ADL: Activities of daily living
AFB: American Foundation for the Blind
AFDC: Aid to Families with Dependent Children; former name for Temporary Assistance for
    Needy Families (TANF)
ALD: Assistive listening device
ALJ: Administrative law judge
APA: American Psychiatric Association
AS: Asperger's syndrome
ASD: Autism spectrum disorders
ASHA: American Speech & Hearing Association
ASL: American Sign Language
AT: Assistive technology
ATBCB: Architectural and Transportation Barriers Compliance Board
BI: Brain injury
C&G: Counseling and guidance
CANAR: Consortia of Administrators for Native American Rehabilitation
CAP: Client Assistance Program
CARF: Commission on Accreditation of Rehabilitation Facilities
CART: Computer-assisted real-time translation
CBO: Congressional Budget Office [Snelling Center]
CCD: Consortium for Citizens With Disabilities
CDC: Centers for Disease Control and Prevention
CFR: Code of Federal Regulations
CI: Cochlear implant
CIL: Center for Independent Living
COBRA: Comprehensive Omnibus Reconciliation Act of 1986
CP: Cerebral palsy
CRC: Certified rehabilitation counselor
CRP: Community rehabilitation program
CSAVR: Council of State Administrators of Vocational Rehabilitation
CSNA: Comprehensive statewide needs assessment
CSPD: Comprehensive System of Personnel Development
DD: Developmental disability

DDS: Disability determination services
DOE: Department of Education
DOL: Department of Labor
DOT: Department of Transportation
DRS: Department of Rehabilitation Services
DSU: Designated state unit
EDGAR: Education Department General Administrative Regulations
EEOC: Equal Employment Opportunity Commission
ESL: English as a Second Language
FERPA: Family Educational Rights and Privacy Act
FY: Fiscal year
GA: General assistance
GAO: Government Accountability Office
GSA: General Services Administration
HI: Hearing Impairment
HLAA: Hearing Loss Association of America
HMO: Health Maintenance Organization
HRD: Human resources development
I&R: Information and referral
ID: Intellectual disability
IDEA: Individuals with Disabilities Education Act
IEP: Individual education plan/program
IHO: Impartial hearing officer
IL: Independent living
ILC: Independent Living Center
IPE: Individualized plan for employment
IM: Information Memorandum
IRI: Institute on Rehabilitation Issues
IRWE: Impairment-related work expense
JAN: Job Accommodations Network
JWOD: Javits-Wagner-O'Day Act
LD: Learning Disability
LPC: Licensed professional counselor
MIS: Management information systems
MOE: Maintenance of effort
MSW: Master of social work
NAD: National Association for the Deaf
NAMI: National Association of Mentally Ill
NAPAS: National Association of Protection and Advocacy System
NCD: National Council on Disability
NCIL: National Council on Independent Living
NCRE: National Council on Rehabilitation Education
NCSAB: National Council of State Administrators for the Blind and Visually Impaired
The NET: the National Employment Team
NFB: National Federation for the Blind
NI: Neurologically impaired

NIDRR: National Institute on Disability and Rehabilitation Research
NRA: National Rehabilitation Association
NRCA: National Rehabilitation Counseling Association
O&M: Orientation and mobility
ODEP: Office of Disability Employment Policy
OJT: On-the-job training
OMB: Office of Management and Budget
OSEP: Office of Special Education Programs
OSERS: Office of Special Education and Rehabilitation Services (Federal)
OSS or OOS: Order of selection for services
OT: Occupational therapy
P&A: Protection and advocacy
PAAT: Protection and advocacy for assistive technology
PADD: Protection and advocacy for persons with developmental disabilities
PAIMI: Protection and advocacy for individuals with mental illness
PAIR: Protection and advocacy for individual rights
PASS: Plan for achieving self-support
PD: Program Directive
PDD: Pervasive developmental disorder not otherwise specified
PreETS: Pre Employment Transition Services
PT: Physical therapy
PVE: Prevocational evaluation
RCD: Rehabilitation counselor for the deaf and hard of hearing
RFP: Request for proposal
RSA: Rehabilitation Services Administration
SCD: Statewide coordinator of services for the deaf and hard of hearing
SCI: Spinal cord injury
SE: Supported employment
SGA: Substantial gainful activity
SILC: State Independent Living Council
SP: State Plan
SPAN: Special Parents Access Network
SPIL: State plan for independent living
SRC: State Rehabilitation Council
SSA: Social Security Administration
SSDI: Social Security Disability Insurance
SSI: Supplemental Security income
TAC: Technical Assistance Circular
TANF: Temporary Assistance for Needy Families
TBI: Traumatic brain injury
TTY: Text telephone
TWP: Trial work period
TWWIIA: Ticket to Work and Work Incentives Improvement Act
UCP: United cerebral palsy
USC: United States code
VA: Veterans' Administration

VR: Vocational rehabilitation
VRS: Vocational Rehabilitation Services
VSA: Very Special Arts
WIOA: Workforce Innovation and Opportunities Act
YES: Youth employment services

Appendix C:

Code of Federal Regulations, Title 34, Part 361-
State Vocational Rehabilitation Services Program

Only where it mentions State Rehabilitation Councils –
This does not constitute binding legal advice.

Prepared by Linda Vegoe and Teesha Kirschbaum

361.5 (2)(v) Administrative Costs

(2) Administrative costs under the vocational rehabilitation services portion of the Unified or Combined State Plan means expenditures incurred in the performance of administrative functions under the vocational rehabilitation program carried out under this part, including expenses related to program planning, development, monitoring, and evaluation, including, but not limited to, expenses for— (v) The State Rehabilitation Council and other advisory committees;

Plain English Summary: Explains where the funding for the SRC comes from. It is part of administrative costs.

361.5(24)(i) Impartial Hearing Officer

(24) Impartial hearing officer.
    (i) Impartial hearing officer means an individual who—
        (A) Is not an employee of a public agency (other than an administrative law judge, hearing examiner, or employee of an institution of higher education);
        (B) Is not a member of the State Rehabilitation Council for the designated State unit;

Plain English Summary
(A) Explains that impartial hearing officers have to be impartial and cannot work for the VR agency or be a member of the SRC.
(B) Emphasizes SRC role in selection of IHO to ensure impartiality.

§361.16 Establishment of an independent commission or a State Rehabilitation Council.

(a) General requirement. Except as provided in paragraph (b) of this section, the vocational rehabilitation services portion of the Unified or Combined State Plan must contain one of the following two assurances:
    (1) An assurance that the designated State agency is an independent State commission that—
        (i) Is responsible under State law for operating, or overseeing the operation of, the vocational rehabilitation program in the State and is primarily concerned with vocational rehabilitation or vocational and other rehabilitation services, in accordance with §361.13(a)(1)(i);
        (ii) Is consumer-controlled by persons who—
            (A) Are individuals with physical or mental impairments that substantially limit major life activities; and
            (B) Represent individuals with a broad range of disabilities, unless the designated State unit under the direction of the commission is the State agency for individuals who are blind;
        (iii) Includes family members, advocates, or other representatives of individuals with mental impairments; and
        (iv) Conducts the functions identified in §361.17(h)(4).
    (2) An assurance that—

(i) The State has established a State Rehabilitation Council (Council) that meets the requirements of §361.17;

(ii) The designated State unit, in accordance with §361.29, jointly develops, agrees to, and reviews annually State goals and priorities and jointly submits to the Secretary annual reports of progress with the Council;

(iii) The designated State unit regularly consults with the Council regarding the development, implementation, and revision of State policies and procedures of general applicability pertaining to the provision of vocational rehabilitation services;

(iv) The designated State unit transmits to the Council—

(A) All plans, reports, and other information required under this part to be submitted to the Secretary;

(B) All policies and information on all practices and procedures of general applicability provided to or used by rehabilitation personnel providing vocational rehabilitation services under this part; and

(C) Copies of due process hearing decisions issued under this part and transmitted in a manner to ensure that the identity of the participants in the hearings is kept confidential; and

(v) The vocational rehabilitation services portion of the Unified or Combined State Plan, and any revision to the vocational rehabilitation services portion of the Unified or Combined State Plan, includes a summary of input provided by the Council, including recommendations from the annual report of the Council, the review and analysis of consumer satisfaction described in §361.17(h)(4), and other reports prepared by the Council, and the designated State unit's response to the input and recommendations, including its reasons for rejecting any input or recommendation of the Council.

(b) Exception for separate State agency for individuals who are blind. In the case of a State that designates a separate State agency under §361.13(a)(3) to administer the part of the vocational rehabilitation services portion of the Unified or Combined State Plan under which vocational rehabilitation services are provided to individuals who are blind, the State must either establish a separate State Rehabilitation Council for each agency that does not meet the requirements in paragraph (a)(1) of this section or establish one State Rehabilitation Council for both agencies if neither agency meets the requirements of paragraph (a)(1) of this section. (Approved by the Office of Management and Budget under control number 1205-0522) (Authority: Sections 101(a)(21) of the Rehabilitation Act of 1973, as amended; 29 U.S.C. 721(a)(21))

Plain English Summary: Each DSU must have either a commission or an SRC that is consumer controlled by individuals with disabilities. This is to ensure there is consumer involvement in the VR program. Cross-disability representation is needed to reflect the diverse needs of the disability community.

Assurances: Explains the SRC involvement with the DSU on State goals, priorities and annual progress reports to the Secretary of the Department of Education (DOE). DSU consults with SRC about state policies and procedures regarding VR services. Describes some of the information the DSU shares with the SRC: such as policies, proposed policies, most information shared with RSA, copies of due process hearing decisions. An assurance that the SRC has a voice for recommendations in the VR portion of the state plan. It cements the SRC's role in providing recommendations in the VR portion of the state plan. Typically, there is an SRC for a general VR program and an SRC for a Blind VR program. The regulations do allow one SRC to represent both programs.

§361.17 (a-g) Requirements for a State Rehabilitation Council.

If the State has established a Council under §361.16(a)(2) or (b), the Council must meet the following requirements:

(a) Appointment.

(1) The members of the Council must be appointed by the Governor or, in the case of a State

that, under State law, vests authority for the administration of the activities carried out under this part in an entity other than the Governor (such as one or more houses of the State legislature or an independent board), the chief officer of that entity.

(2) The appointing authority must select members of the Council after soliciting recommendations from representatives of organizations representing a broad range of individuals with disabilities and organizations interested in individuals with disabilities. In selecting members, the appointing authority must consider, to the greatest extent practicable, the extent to which minority populations are represented on the Council.

(b) Composition.

(1) General. Except as provided in paragraph (b)(3) of this section, the Council must be composed of at least 15 members, including—

(i) At least one representative of the Statewide Independent Living Council, who must be the chairperson or other designee of the Statewide Independent Living Council;

(ii) At least one representative of a parent training and information center established pursuant to section 682(a) of the Individuals with Disabilities Education Act;

(iii) At least one representative of the Client Assistance Program established under part 370 of this

chapter, who must be the director of or other individual recommended by the Client Assistance Program;

(iv) At least one qualified vocational rehabilitation counselor with knowledge of and experience with vocational rehabilitation programs who serves as an ex officio, nonvoting member of the Council if employed by the designated State agency;

(v) At least one representative of community rehabilitation program service providers;

(vi) Four representatives of business, industry, and labor;

(vii) Representatives of disability groups that include a cross section of—

(A) Individuals with physical, cognitive, sensory, and mental disabilities; and

(B) Representatives of individuals with disabilities who have difficulty representing themselves or are unable due to their disabilities to represent themselves;

(viii) Current or former applicants for, or recipients of, vocational rehabilitation services;

(ix) In a State in which one or more projects are funded under section 121 of the Act (American Indian Vocational Rehabilitation Services), at least one representative of the directors of the projects in such State;

(x) At least one representative of the State educational agency responsible for the public education of students with disabilities who are eligible to receive services under this part and part B of the Individuals with Disabilities Education Act;

(xi) At least one representative of the State workforce development board; and

(xii) The director of the designated State unit as an ex officio, nonvoting member of the Council.

(2) Employees of the designated State agency. Employees of the designated State agency may serve only as nonvoting members of the Council. This provision does not apply to the representative appointed pursuant to paragraph (b)(1)(iii) of this section.

(3) Composition of a separate Council for a separate State agency for individuals who are blind. Except as provided in paragraph (b)(4) of this section, if the State establishes a separate Council for a separate State agency for individuals who are blind, that Council must—

(i) Conform with all of the composition requirements for a Council under paragraph (b)(1) of this section, except the requirements in paragraph (b)(1)(vii), unless the exception in paragraph (b)(4) of this section applies; and

(ii) Include—

(A) At least one representative of a disability advocacy group representing individuals who are blind; and

(B) At least one representative of an individual who is blind, has multiple disabilities, and has difficulty representing himself or herself or is unable due to disabilities to represent himself or herself.

(4) Exception. If State law in effect on October 29, 1992 requires a separate Council under paragraph (b)(3) of this section to have fewer than 15 members, the separate Council is in compliance with the composition requirements in paragraphs (b)(1)(vi) and (b)(1)(viii) of this section if it includes at least one representative who meets the requirements for each of those paragraphs.

(c) Majority.

(1) A majority of the Council members must be individuals with disabilities who meet the requirements of §361.5(c)(28) and are not employed by the designated State unit.

(2) In the case of a separate Council established under §361.16(b), a majority of the Council members must be individuals who are blind and are not employed by the designated State unit.

(d) Chairperson.

(1) The chairperson must be selected by the members of the Council from among the voting members of the Council, subject to the veto power of the Governor; or

(2) In States in which the Governor does not have veto power pursuant to State law, the appointing authority described in paragraph (a)(1) of this section must designate a member of the Council to serve as the chairperson of the Council or must require the Council to designate a member to serve as chairperson.

(e) Terms of appointment.

(1) Each member of the Council must be appointed for a term of no more than three years, and each member of the Council, other than a representative identified in paragraph (b)(1)(iii) or (ix) of this section, may serve for no more than two consecutive full terms.

(2) A member appointed to fill a vacancy occurring prior to the end of the term for which the predecessor was appointed must be appointed for the remainder of the predecessor's term.

(3) The terms of service of the members initially appointed must be, as specified by the appointing authority as described in paragraph (a)(1) of this section, for varied numbers of years to ensure that terms expire on a staggered basis.

(f) Vacancies.

(1) A vacancy in the membership of the Council must be filled in the same manner as the original appointment, except the appointing authority as described in paragraph (a)(1) of this section may delegate the authority to fill that vacancy to the remaining members of the Council after making the original appointment.

(2) No vacancy affects the power of the remaining members to execute the duties of the Council.

(g) Conflict of interest. No member of the Council may cast a vote on any matter that would provide direct financial benefit to the member or the member's organization or otherwise give the appearance of a conflict of interest under State law.

Plain English Summary: SRC members must be appointed by the Governor, unless the Governor has designated someone else.

Gives a description of the make-up of the SRC. Number of members (minimum 15) and what groups must be represented. The Rehab Act is very prescriptive on who must be on the SRC. It is supposed to represent both the disability and business community. Provides some clarity on compositions differences between a General SRC and a Blind SRC. At least 51% of SRC members must be individuals with disabilities. This demonstrates that the voice of individuals with disabilities is heard. SRC must elect its own chair, the -Governor does have veto power over the chair position. Explains terms of appointment. Terms are 3 years long, with the possibility of two terms. CAP and Tribal VR representative do not have term limits. State Director position-does not have a term limit. It is filled by whoever is sitting in that position, they do still have to be appointed. State Director and VRC position (if employed by DSU) are non voting members. Explains that no vacancy stops the SRC from completing its work. No member can have a conflict of interest. Such as having a direct financial benefit to you, your organization or someone related to you. It also includes the appearance of a conflict of interest.

(1) Review, analyze, and advise the designated State unit regarding the performance of the State unit's responsibilities under this part, particularly responsibilities related to—
    (i) Eligibility, including order of selection;
    (ii) The extent, scope, and effectiveness of services provided; and
    (iii) Functions performed by State agencies that affect or potentially affect the ability of individuals with disabilities in achieving employment outcomes under this part;

Plain English Summary
We review, analyze and advise so we can make good recommendations. In order to do that we need information. DSU gives the data needed to provide feedback on eligibility, Order of Selection (OOS), services, ability of customers to achieve employment outcomes.

(2) In partnership with the designated State unit—
    (i) Develop, agree to, and review State goals and priorities in accordance with § 361.29(c); and
    (ii) Evaluate the effectiveness of the vocational rehabilitation program and submit reports of progress to the Secretary in accordance with § 361.29(e);

Plain English Summary: Second time it mentions that SRCs work jointly with the DSU on state goals and priorities and progress reports to RSA.

(3) Advise the designated State agency and the designated State unit regarding activities carried out under this part and assist in the preparation of the vocational rehabilitation services portion of the Unified or Combined State Plan and amendments to the plan, applications, reports, needs assessments, and evaluations required by this part;

Plain English Summary
The SRC has a large role in the VR portion of the state plan creation, CSNA and other evaluation duties of the DSU.

(4) To the extent feasible, conduct a review and analysis of the effectiveness of, and consumer satisfaction with—
    (i) The functions performed by the designated State agency;
    (ii) The vocational rehabilitation services provided by State agencies and other public and private entities responsible for providing vocational rehabilitation services to individuals with disabilities under the Act; and
    (iii) The employment outcomes achieved by eligible individuals receiving services under this part, including the availability of health and other employment benefits in connection with those employment outcomes;

Plain English Summary
As much as the SRC can-they review and analyze how well the DSU is doing and the satisfaction level of VR customers regarding to the DSU's functions. This is usually done with a customer satisfaction survey. SRC have much latitude in how they complete their customer satisfaction surveys.

(5) Prepare and submit to the Governor and to the Secretary no later than 90 days after the end of

the Federal fiscal year an annual report on the status of vocational rehabilitation programs operated within the State and make the report available to the public through appropriate modes of communication;

Plain English Summary

By December 31st of each year SRCs send an Annual Report to the Secretary of DOE and the Governor. [in practice this involves sending the annual report to your RSA State Liaison]. It's a status report of VR services. This report has to be made public.

361.17 (h)(6)

(6) Coordinate activities with the activities of other councils, including the Statewide Independent Living Council established under chapter 1, title VII of the Act, the advisory panel established under section 612(a)(21) of the Individuals with Disabilities Education Act, the State Developmental Disabilities Planning Council described in section 124 of the Developmental Disabilities Assistance and Bill of Rights Act, the State mental health planning council established under section 1914(a) of the Public Health Service Act, and the State workforce development board, and with the activities of entities carrying out programs under the Assistive Technology Act of 1998;

Plain English Summary

The SRC is expected to have a partnership with each of these organizations. Find out who they are in your state.

361.17 (h)(7)

(7) Provide for coordination and the establishment of working relationships between the designated State agency and the Statewide Independent Living Council and centers for independent living within the State; and

Plain English Summary

The SRC could help foster a working relationship between the SILC and CILs. SRC should be aware of Independent Living activities in their state.

361.17 (h)(8)

(8) Perform other comparable functions, consistent with the purpose of this part, as the Council determines to be appropriate, that are comparable to the other functions performed by the Council.

Plain English Summary

The SRC has the opportunity to determine other activities that would further their involvement and opportunity for partnership and/or input with regard to the VR system in their state.

371.17 (i)

(i) *Resources.*

(1) The Council, in conjunction with the designated State unit, must prepare a plan for the provision of resources, including staff and other personnel that may be necessary and sufficient for the Council to carry out its functions under this part.

(2) The resource plan must, to the maximum extent possible, rely on the use of resources in existence during the period of implementation of the plan.

(3) Any disagreements between the designated State unit and the Council regarding the amount of resources necessary to carry out the functions of the Council must be resolved by the Governor, consistent with paragraphs (i)(1) and (2) of this section.

(4) The Council must, consistent with State law, supervise and evaluate the staff and personnel that are necessary to carry out its functions.

(5) Those staff and personnel that are assisting the Council in carrying out its functions may not be assigned duties by the designated State unit or any other agency or office of the State that would create a conflict of interest.

Plain English Summary

The SRC is required to do a Resource Plan, which lists resources necessary for its operation such as staff and other personnel. It should rely on current resources.

Disagreements on required resources must be resolved by the Governor.

The Council must, in accordance with state law, supervise SRC staff and personnel. (This does not include merit system staff)

The SRC staff must avoid conflicts of interest by not carrying out duties assigned by the DSU or other state agency that would create a conflict.

371.17 (j)

(j) *Meetings.* The Council must—

(1) Convene at least four meetings a year in locations determined by the Council to be necessary to conduct Council business. The meetings must be publicly announced, open, and accessible to the general public, including individuals with disabilities, unless there is a valid reason for an executive session; and

(2) Conduct forums or hearings, as appropriate, that are publicly announced, open, and accessible to the public, including individuals with disabilities.

Plain English Summary

371.17 (k)

(k) *Compensation.* Funds appropriated under Title I of the Act, except funds to carry out sections 112 and 121 of the Act, may be used to compensate and reimburse the expenses of Council members in accordance with section 105(g) of the Act.

Plain English Summary

361.18 Comprehensive system of personnel development.

The vocational rehabilitation services portion of the Unified or Combined State Plan must describe the procedures and activities the State agency will undertake to establish and maintain a comprehensive system of personnel development designed to ensure an adequate supply of qualified rehabilitation personnel, including professionals and paraprofessionals, for the designated State unit. If the State agency has a State Rehabilitation Council, this description must, at a minimum, specify that the Council has an opportunity to review and comment on the development of plans, policies, and procedures necessary to meet the requirements of paragraphs (b) through (d) of this section.

Plain English Summary

The VR Portion of the State Plan must include a section on the Comprehensive System of Personnel Development (CSPD) that describes actions by the State agency to ensure a sufficient number of qualified VR counselors; this section must also contain an assurance that the SRC had an opportunity to comment on the CSPD.

361.20 Public Participation Requirements

(b) Notice requirements. The vocational rehabilitation services portion of the Unified or Combined State Plan must assure that the designated State agency, prior to conducting the public meetings, provides appropriate and sufficient notice throughout the State of the meetings in accordance with—

(1) State law governing public meetings; or

(2) In the absence of State law governing public meetings, procedures developed by the designated State agency in consultation with the State Rehabilitation Council.

(c) Summary of input of the State Rehabilitation Council.

The vocational rehabilitation services portion of the Unified or Combined State Plan must provide a summary of the input of the State Rehabilitation Council, if the State agency has a Council, into the vocational rehabilitation services portion of the Unified or Combined State Plan and any amendment to that portion of the plan, in accordance with §361.16(a)(2)(v).

(d) Special consultation requirements. The vocational rehabilitation services portion of the Unified Combined State Plan must assure that the State agency actively consults with the director of the Client Assistance Program, the State Rehabilitation Council, if the State agency has a Council, and, as appropriate, Indian tribes, tribal organizations, and native Hawaiian organizations on its policies and procedures governing the provision of vocational rehabilitation services under the vocational rehabilitation services portion of the Unified or Combined State Plan.

Plain English Summary

The State agency must provide sufficient notice of the State Plan public hearings. The VR portion of the State plan must include a summary of SRC input. The VR portion of the State Plan must contain assurances that the State agency consulted with the CAP, SRC, and Indian organizations on VR policies and procedures.

361.21 Consultations regarding the administration of the vocational rehabilitation services portion of the Unified or Combined State plan.

The vocational rehabilitation services portion of the Unified or Combined State Plan must assure that, in connection with matters of general policy arising in the administration of the vocational rehabilitation services portion of the Unified or Combined State Plan, the designated State agency takes into account the views of—

(a) Individuals and groups of individuals who are recipients of vocational rehabilitation services or, as appropriate, the individuals' representatives;

(b) Personnel working in programs that provide vocational rehabilitation services to individuals with disabilities;

(c) Providers of vocational rehabilitation services to individuals with disabilities;

(d) The director of the Client Assistance Program; and

(e) The State Rehabilitation Council, if the State has a Council.

Plain English Summary

The VR portion of the State Plan must contain assurances that the State agency in creating general VR policy takes into account the input of VR clients or their representatives, program personnel who provide VR services, VR service providers (like CRPs), CAP director and the SRC.

361.29 Statewide assessment; annual estimates; annual State goals and priorities; strategies; and progress reports.

(a) Comprehensive statewide assessment.

(1) The vocational rehabilitation services portion of the Unified Combined State Plan must

include—

(i) The results of a comprehensive, statewide assessment, jointly conducted by the designated State unit and the State Rehabilitation Council (if the State unit has a Council) every three years. Results of the assessment are to be included in the vocational rehabilitation portion of the Unified or Combined State Plan, submitted in accordance with the requirements of §361.10(a) and the joint regulations of this part. The comprehensive needs assessment must describe the rehabilitation needs of individuals with disabilities residing within the State, particularly the vocational rehabilitation services needs of—

(A) Individuals with the most significant disabilities, including their need for supported employment services;

(B) Individuals with disabilities who are minorities and individuals with disabilities who have been unserved or underserved by the vocational rehabilitation program carried out under this part;

(C) Individuals with disabilities served through other components of the statewide workforce development system as identified by those individuals and personnel assisting those individuals through the components of the system; and

(D) Youth with disabilities, and students with disabilities, including

(1) Their need for pre-employment transition services or other transition services; and

(2) An assessment of the needs of individuals with disabilities for transition services and pre-employment transition services, and the extent to which such services provided under this part are coordinated with transition services provided under the Individuals with Disabilities Education Act (20 U.S.C. 1400 et seq.) in order to meet the needs of individuals with disabilities.

(ii) An assessment of the need to establish, develop, or improve community rehabilitation programs within the State.

(2) The vocational rehabilitation services portion of the Unified or Combined State Plan must assure that the State will submit to the Secretary a report containing information regarding updates to the assessments under paragraph (a) of this section for any year in which the State updates the assessments at such time and in such manner as the Secretary determines appropriate.

(b) Annual estimates. The vocational rehabilitation services portion of the Unified or Combined State Plan must include, and must assure that the State will submit a report to the Secretary (at such time and in such manner determined appropriate by the Secretary) that includes, State estimates of—

(1) The number of individuals in the State who are eligible for services under this part;

(2) The number of eligible individuals who will receive services provided with funds provided under this part and under part §363, including, if the designated State Plan must identify the State's service and outcome goals and the time within which these goals may be achieved for individuals in each priority category within the order.

(c) *Goals and priorities*—

(1) *In general.* The State plan must identify the goals and priorities of the State in carrying out the program.

(2) *Council.* The goals and priorities must be jointly developed, agreed to, reviewed annually, and, as necessary, revised by the designated State unit and the State Rehabilitation Council, if the State unit has a Council.

(3) *Submission.* The State plan must assure that the State will submit to the Secretary a report containing information regarding revisions in the goals and priorities for any year in which the State revises the goals and priorities.

(4) *Basis for goals and priorities.* The State goals and priorities must be based on an analysis of—

(i) The comprehensive statewide assessment described in paragraph (a) of this section, including any updates to the assessment;

(ii) The performance of the State on the standards and indicators established under section 106 of the Act; and

(iii) Other available information on the operation and the effectiveness of the vocational rehabilitation program carried out in the State, including any reports received from the State Rehabilitation Council under §361.17(h) and the findings and recommendations from monitoring activities conducted under section 107 of the Act.

(5) *Service and outcome goals for categories in order of selection.* If the designated State agency uses an order of selection in accordance with §361.36, the State plan must identify the State's service and outcome goals and the time within which these goals may be achieved for individuals in each priority category within the order.

(d) Strategies. The vocational rehabilitation services portion of the Unified or Combined State Plan must describe the strategies the State will use to address the needs identified in the assessment conducted under paragraph (a) of this section and achieve the goals and priorities identified in paragraph (c) of this section, including—

(1) The methods to be used to expand and improve to individuals with disabilities, including how a broad range of assistive technology services and assistive technology devices will be provided to those individuals at each stage of the rehabilitation process and how those services and devices will be provided to individuals with disabilities on a statewide basis;

(2) The methods to be used to improve and expand vocational rehabilitation services for students with disabilities, including the coordination of services designed to facilitate the transition of such students from the receipt of educational services in school to postsecondary life, including the receipt of vocational rehabilitation services under the Act, postsecondary education, employment, and pre-employment transition services;

(3) Strategies developed and implemented by the State to address the needs of students and youth with disabilities identified in the assessments described in paragraph (a) of this section and strategies to achieve the goals and priorities identified by the State to improve and expand vocational rehabilitation services for students and youth with disabilities on a statewide basis;

(4) Strategies to provide pre-employment transition services;

(5) Outreach procedures to identify and serve individuals with disabilities who are minorities and individuals with disabilities who have been unserved or by the vocational rehabilitation program;

(6) As applicable, the plan of the State for establishing, developing, or improving community rehabilitation programs;

(7) Strategies to improve the performance of the State with respect to the evaluation standards and performance indicators established pursuant to section 106 of the Act and section 116 of Workforce Innovation and Act; and

(8) Strategies for assisting other components of the statewide workforce development system in assisting individuals with disabilities.

(e) Evaluation and reports of progress.

(1) The vocational rehabilitation services portion of the Unified or Combined State Plan must include—

(i) The results of an evaluation of the effectiveness of the vocational rehabilitation program; and

(ii) A joint report by the designated State unit and the State Rehabilitation Council, if the State unit has a Council, to the Secretary on the progress made in improving the effectiveness of the program from the previous year. This evaluation and joint report must include—

(A) An evaluation of the extent to which the goals and priorities identified in paragraph (c) of this section were achieved;

(B) A description of the strategies that contributed to the achievement of the goals and priorities;

(C) To the extent to which the goals and priorities were not achieved, a description of the factors that impeded that achievement; and

(D) An assessment of the performance of the State on the standards and indicators established pursuant to section 106 of the Act.

(2) The vocational rehabilitation services portion of the Unified or Combined State Plan must assure that the designated State unit and the State Rehabilitation Council, if the State unit has a Council, will jointly submit to the Secretary a report that contains the information described in paragraph (e)(1) of this section at such time and in such manner the Secretary determines appropriate.

Plain English Summary

The SRC with the VR Agency conducts a comprehensive statewide needs assessment (CSNA) for the state plan every 3 yrs. The CSNA looks at a number of things including needs of individuals who are most significantly disabled, needs of unserved or underserved, transition and Pre ETS, and the need for CRP's. For additional areas, please see the regulations.

The state plan should identify the State's services, outcome goals, and the planned achievement of those goals.

The plan requires strategies to address areas in the CSNA, and how to achieve the goals and priorities. This includes methods used to reach the goals. The SRC works with VR to provide a progress report of the improvement of the VR program from the previous year, which is submitted to the Secretary of Education.

361.35 Innovation and expansion activities.

(a) The vocational rehabilitation services portion of the Unified or Combined State Plan must assure that the State will reserve and use a portion of the funds allotted to the State under section 110 of the Act—

(1) For the development and implementation of innovative approaches to expand and improve the provision of vocational rehabilitation services to individuals with disabilities, particularly individuals with the most significant disabilities, including transition services for students and youth with disabilities and pre-employment services for students with disabilities, consistent with the findings of the comprehensive statewide assessment of the rehabilitation needs of individuals with disabilities under §361.29(a) and the State's goals and priorities under §361.29(c);

(2) To support the funding of—

(i) The State Rehabilitation Council, if the State has a Council, consistent with the resource plan identified in §361.17(i); and

(ii) The Statewide Independent Living Council, consistent with the plan prepared under 34 CFR 364.21(i).

(b) The State plan must—

(1) Describe how the reserved funds will be used; and

(2) Include, on an annual basis, a report describing how the reserved funds were used during the preceding year.

Plain English Summary

Innovation and expansion funds can be used for the following:

Innovative approaches to serve individuals with the most significant disabilities, including transition students and youth

Support funding of the State Rehabilitation Council

Support funding of the State Independent Living Council

361.36 Innovation and expansion activities. (f) State Rehabilitation Council.

(f)The designated State unit must consult with the State Rehabilitation Council, if the State unit has a Council, regarding the—

    (1) Need to establish an order of selection, including any reevaluation of the need under paragraph (c)(2) of this section;

    (2) Priority categories of the particular order of selection;

    (3) Criteria for determining individuals with the most significant disabilities; and

    (4) Administration of the order of selection.

Plain English Summary

The VR program must consult with SRC regarding; 1) order of selection (OOS), 2) priority categories of the OOS, 3) criteria for determining individuals with the most significant disabilities, administration of the order of selection.

361.47 Records of Service (b)

(b) The State unit, in consultation with the State Rehabilitation Council if the State has a Council, must determine the type of documentation that the State unit must maintain for each applicant and eligible individual in order to meet the requirements in paragraph (a) of this section.

Plain English Summary

361.52 Informed Choice (b)

(a) *General provision.* The State plan must assure that applicants and eligible individuals or, as appropriate, their representatives are provided information and support services to assist applicants and eligible individuals in exercising informed choice throughout the rehabilitation process consistent with the provisions of section 102(d) of the Act and the requirements of this section.

(b) *Written policies and procedures.* The designated State unit, in consultation with its State Rehabilitation Council, if it has a Council, must develop and implement written policies and procedures that enable an applicant or eligible individual to exercise informed choice throughout the vocational rehabilitation process. These policies and procedures must provide for—

    (1) Informing each applicant and eligible individual (including students with disabilities who are making the transition from programs under the responsibility of an educational agency to programs under the responsibility of the designated State unit), through appropriate modes of communication, about the availability of and opportunities to exercise informed choice, including the availability of support services for individuals with cognitive or other disabilities who require assistance in exercising informed choice throughout the vocational rehabilitation process;

    (2) Assisting applicants and eligible individuals in exercising informed choice in decisions related to the provision of assessment services;

    (3) Developing and implementing flexible procurement policies and methods that facilitate the provision of vocational rehabilitation services and that afford eligible individuals meaningful choices among the methods used to procure vocational rehabilitation services;

    (4) Assisting eligible individuals or, as appropriate, the individuals' representatives in acquiring information that enables them to exercise informed choice in the development of their IPEs with respect to the selection of the—

        (i) Employment outcome;

        (ii) Specific vocational rehabilitation services needed to achieve the employment outcome;

        (iii) Entity that will provide the services;

        (iv) Employment setting and the settings in which the services will be provided; and

        (v) Methods available for procuring the services; and

    (5) Ensuring that the availability and scope of informed choice is consistent with the obligations of the designated State agency under this part.

Plain English Summary

361.57 Review of determinations made by designated State unit personnel. (f)(ii)

(a) *Procedures.* The designated State unit must develop and implement procedures to ensure that an applicant or eligible individual who is dissatisfied with any determination made by personnel of the designated State unit that affects the provision of vocational rehabilitation services may request, or, if appropriate, may request through the individual's representative, a timely review of that determination. The procedures must be in accordance with paragraphs (b) through (k) of this section:

(f) Selection of impartial hearing officers. The impartial hearing officer for a particular case must be selected —

(1) From a list of qualified impartial hearing officers maintained by the State unit. Impartial hearing officers included on the list must be—

(i) Identified by the State unit if the State unit is an independent commission; or

(ii) Jointly identified by the State unit and the State Rehabilitation Council if the State has a Council;

Plain English Summary

Impartial Hearing Officers (IHO) are randomly selected from a list of IHO's that are jointly identified by VR and the SRC.

Appendix D:
Introduction to Robert's Rules of Order

What is parliamentary procedure?
It is a set of rules for conduct at meetings that allows everyone to be heard and to make decisions without confusion.

Why is parliamentary procedure important?
Because it's a time-tested method of conducting business at meetings and public gatherings. It can be adapted to fit the needs of any organization. Today, Robert's Rules of Order newly revised is the basic handbook of operation for most clubs, organizations, and other groups. So it's important that everyone know these basic rules!

Organizations using parliamentary procedure usually follow a fixed order of business. Below is a typical example:

- Call to order
- Roll call of members present
- Reading of minutes of last meeting
- Officers' reports
- Committee reports
- Special orders: Important business previously designated for consideration at this meeting
- Unfinished business
- New business
- Announcements
- Adjournment

The method used by members to express themselves is in the form of moving motions. A motion is a proposal that the entire membership can take action on or a stand on an issue. Individual members can

- Call to order
- Second motions
- Debate motions
- Vote on motions

There are four basic types of motions:

- *Main motions:* The purpose of a main motion is to introduce items to the membership for their consideration. Main motions cannot be made when any other motion is on the floor and yield to privileged, subsidiary, and incidental motions.
- *Subsidiary motions:* Their purpose is to change or affect how a main motion is handled, and they are voted on before a main motion.
- *Privileged motions:* Their purpose is to bring up items that are urgent about special or important matters unrelated to pending business.
- *Incidental motions:* Their purpose is to provide a means of questioning procedure concerning other motions, and they must be considered before the other motion.

How are motions presented?

1. *Obtain the floor.*
    a. Wait until the last speaker has finished.
    b. Rise and address the chairman by saying "Mr. Chairman" or "Mr. President."
    c. Wait until the chairman recognizes you.
2. *Make your motion.*
    a. Speak in a clear and concise manner.
    b. Always state a motion affirmatively. Say, "I move that we . . ." rather than "I move that we do not. . . ."
    c. Avoid personalities and stay on your subject.
3. *Wait for someone to second your motion.*
4. *Another member will second your motion or the chairman will call for a second.*

5. *If there is no second to your motion, it is lost.*
6. *The chairman states your motion.*
    a. The chairman will say, "It has been moved and seconded that we . . ." thus placing your motion before the membership for consideration and action.
    b. The membership then either debates your motion or may move directly to a vote.
    c. Once your motion is presented to the membership by the chairman, it becomes "assembly property" and cannot be changed by you without the consent of the members.
7. *Expanding on your motion*
    a. The time for you to speak in favor of your motion is at this point in time, rather than at the time you present it.
    b. The mover is always allowed to speak first.
    c. All comments and debate must be directed to the chairman.
    d. Keep to the time limit for speaking that has been established.
    e. The mover may speak again only after other speakers are finished, unless called upon by the chairman.
8. *Putting the question to the membership*
    a. The chairman asks, "Are you ready to vote on the question?"
    b. If there is no more discussion, a vote is taken.
    c. On a motion to move the previous question may be adapted.

Voting on a Motion
The method of vote on any motion depends on the situation and the bylaws or policy of your organization. There are five methods used to vote by most organizations:
- *By voice.* The chairman asks those in favor to say "aye" and those opposed to say "no." Any member may move for an exact count.
- *By roll call.* Each member answers "yes" or "no" as his name is called. This method is used when a record of each person's vote is required.
- *By general consent.* When a motion is not likely to be opposed, the chairman says, "If there is no objection . . . " The membership shows agreement by their silence; however, if one member says, "I object," the item must be put to a vote.
- *By division.* This is a slight verification of a voice vote. It does not require a count unless the chairman so desires. Members raise their hands or stand.
- *By ballot.* Members write their vote on a slip of paper. This method is used when secrecy is desired.

Two other motions are commonly used that relate to voting.
- *Motion to table.* This motion is often used in the attempt to "kill" a motion. The option is always present, however, to "take from the table," for reconsideration by the membership.
- *Motion to postpone indefinitely.* This is often used as a means of parliamentary strategy and allows opponents of a motion to test their strength without an actual vote being taken. Also, debate is once again open on the main motion.

Parliamentary procedure is the best way to get things done at your meetings. But, it will only work if you use it properly.

- Allow motions that are in order.
- Have members obtain the floor properly.
- Speak clearly and concisely.
- Obey the rules of debate.

Most importantly, *be courteous!*

The full text of Robert's Rules of Order can be downloaded at http://www.constitution.org/rror/rror--00.htm.

Appendix E:
What Are Other SRCs Doing?
Where Can I Find Examples?

This appendix provides examples of various SRC reports and approaches to formalized SRC organization. There are no prescribed guidelines for these activities, and SRCs therefore often ask for examples from other SRCs. There are many formats and approaches. The following examples are not intended as templates, just individual state approaches.

SRC annual reports and other reports, as well as state structures and other useful information, are available on many individual state agency websites. Links to these can be found on the NCSRC website- www.ncsrc.net.

This appendix has six sections:

Section 1. Example of SRC bylaws (New Jersey)
Section 2: Example of SRC Handbook (New Jersey)
Section 3. Example of SRC operating procedures (Oklahoma)
Section 4. Example of SRC input to state plan (West Virginia)
Section 5. Example of notebook for RSA monitoring visit (West Virginia)
Section 6. Example worksheet: Membership composition mandates (for tracking)

Section 1:
Example of SRC Bylaws

(New Jersey)

Article I – Designation
The Organization referred to in this document shall be known as the State Rehabilitation Council.

Article II – Authorization
The State Rehabilitation Council was established pursuant to section 105 of the 1998 Amendments to the Rehabilitation Act.

Article III – Mission
The State Rehabilitation Council is a partnership of individuals with disabilities, advocates, and other interested persons. It is committed to ensuring, through policy development, implementation, and advocacy, that New Jersey has a state vocational rehabilitation program that is not only comprehensive and consumer-responsive but also effective, efficient, and sufficiently funded. The State Rehabilitation Council is dedicated to ensuring that people with disabilities receive rehabilitation services that result in competitive, integrated employment.

Article IV – Purpose
The Purpose of the Council is to:
1. provide guidance for the development and expansion of vocational rehabilitation services, programs, and concepts on a statewide basis to maximize employability, independence, and integration of people with disabilities into the work force and the community;
2. provide guidance to state agencies and to local planning and administrative entities that affect or potentially affect the ability of people with disabilities to achieve rehabilitation goals and objectives; and
3. advocate for the promotion and expansion of vocational rehabilitation services within the state.

Article V – Duties
The Council shall:
1. review, analyze, and advise the New Jersey Division of Vocational Rehabilitation Services (DVRS) regarding the performance of the responsibilities of the DVRS, particularly responsibilities relating to –
   a. eligibility (including order of selection);
   b. the extent, scope, and effectiveness of services provided; and
   c. functions performed by state agencies that affect or that potentially affect the ability of people with disabilities in achieving employment outcomes under Title I of the Rehabilitation act;
2. In partnership with the DVRS --

    a. develop, agree to, and review state goals and priorities in accordance with section 101 (a) (15) (C); and

    b. evaluate the effectiveness of the vocational rehabilitation program and submit reports of progress to the Commissioner in accordance with section 101 (a) (15) (E);

3. advise the DVRS regarding activities authorized to be carried out under Title I, and assist in the preparation of the State Plan and amendments to the Plan, applications, reports, needs assessments, and evaluations required by Title I;

4. to the extent feasible, conduct a review and analysis of the effectiveness of, and consumer satisfaction with -

    a. the functions performed by the designated State agency;

    b. vocational rehabilitation services provided by state agencies and other public and private entities responsible for providing vocational rehabilitation services to individuals with disabilities under the Act; and

    c. employment outcomes achieved by eligible individuals receiving services under Title I, including the availability of health and other employment benefits in connection with such employment outcomes;

5. prepare and submit an annual report to the Governor and the commissioner on the status of vocational rehabilitation programs operated within the State, and make the report available to the public;

6. to avoid duplication of efforts and enhance the number of individuals served, coordinate activities with the activities of other councils within the State, including the Statewide Independent Living Council established under Chapter 1, title VII of the Act, the advisory panel established under section 612 (a) (21) of the Individual with Disabilities Education Act, the State Developmental Disabilities Planning Council described in section 124 of the Developmental Disabilities Assistance and Bill of rights Act, the State Mental Health Planning Council established under section 1914(a) of the Public Health Service Act, the State workforce development board; with the activities of entities carrying out the programs under the Assistive Technology Act of 1998; and the Commission for the Blind and Visually Impaired State Rehabilitation Council.

7. prepare, in conjunction with the DVRS, a plan for the provision of such resources, including such staff and other personnel, as may be necessary and sufficient to carry out the functions of the Council; and

8. In cooperation with DVRS, assist in the development of reports and recommendations to the Federal entity (RSA) as required by the Rehabilitation Act.

Article VI – Membership

1. Membership shall be in accordance with Section 105 of the 2014 Amendments to the Rehabilitation Act and Executive Order 110 and shall reflect a diverse range of disability groups, geographical areas, racial and ethnic groups and gender and be comprised of the following:

    a. At least one representative of the Statewide Independent Living Council established under section 705, which representative may be the chairperson or other designee of the Council.

    b. At least one representative of a parent training and information center established pursuant to section 682(a) of the Individuals with Disabilities Education Act (as added by section 101 of the Individuals with Disabilities Education act Amendments of 1997; Public Law 105-17);

   c. At least one representative of the Client Assistance Program established under section 112;

   d. At least one qualified vocational rehabilitation counselor with knowledge of and experience with the vocational rehabilitation program who shall serve as an ex officio, non-voting member of the Council if the counselor is an employee of the designated State agency;

   e. At least one representative who is a community rehabilitation program service provider;

   f. Four representatives of business, industry, and labor;

   g. Representatives of disability advocacy groups representing a cross section of—

      i. individuals with physical, cognitive, sensory and mental disabilities; and

      ii. persons who are representatives of individuals with disabilities who have difficulty in representing themselves or are unable due to their disabilities to represent themselves;

   h. Current or former applicants for, or recipients of, vocational rehabilitation services;

   i. At least one representative of the state educational agency responsible for the public education of students with disabilities who are eligible to receive services under title I and part B of the Individuals with Disabilities Education Act;

   j. At least one representative of the state workforce development board; and

   k. The Director of the DVRS shall serve as an ex-officio, non-voting member of the Council.

2. A majority of council members shall be persons with disabilities, not employed by the DVRS.
3. The total number of voting members shall not exceed twenty-five (25).

Article VII – Appointment of Members

1. Members of the Council shall be appointed by the Governor for three- year terms.
2. Members may serve no more than two consecutive full three-year terms, excluding the representative of the Client Assistance Program who has no term limit. In order to be eligible to be reappointed following completion of two consecutive terms, a member must complete a period of two (2) months in non-member status following the last date of the member's second term.
3. Annually, the Executive Committee shall review the membership of the Council and make recommendations for major actions by the council relative to re-nomination or continuance of individual members.
4. Based upon attendance, participation and continuing interest of current members, and other factors as may be appropriate, the Membership Committee shall prepare a list of persons to be recommended to the Governor for appointment or continued service on the Council.

Article VIII – Meetings

1. The Council shall meet at least four times per year.
2. A quorum (fifty percent plus one of appointed members) shall be required for any action requiring a vote.

3. Affirmative vote of fifty percent plus one of quorum members present and voting at the meeting is required for any official Council action.
4. Participation at meetings through alternative technology media shall be allowed when necessary (teleconferencing, video conferencing, etc.)
5. Members may send a representative to attend a meeting, but a proxy vote shall not be allowed and such representatives shall not be included in the quorum.
6. Public Notices shall be given for full council meetings.
7. Special meetings may be called as deemed necessary by the Executive Committee. Notification of not less than five business days shall be made to all members.
8. Council documents shall be provided in alternative format, as requested.
9. Roberts Rules of Order (most recent edition) shall be used as guidance during Council meetings.

Article IX – Officers

1. Officers of the Council shall include a Chairperson, a Vice-Chairperson, and a Treasurer. The Chairperson shall convene the meetings of the Council and preside at the meetings. When the Chairperson is not available, the Vice-Chairperson shall preside. The Vice Chairperson shall be responsible for the development of the Annual Report to Rehabilitation Services Administration (RSA).
2. Officers shall serve a term of two years and shall be eligible for one additional consecutive term.
3. In the event of a vacancy lasting longer than one half of a term of office, a special election shall be held at the next Council meeting.

Article X Election and Terms of Office

1. A nominating committee of a minimum of three voting members, not already holding a council office, shall be appointed by the executive Committee at the November meeting of the non-election year. The committee shall develop a recommended slate of officers for consideration by the Council at the following May meeting. The names of those recommended shall be sent to all members with the meeting notice for the May meeting.
2. At the second meeting of the election year, the slate recommended by the nominating committee as well as nominations made from the floor shall be considered, and an election held. A majority vote of the members present shall be required for election. (Quorum required.)

Article XI – Executive Committee

1. The current officers, immediate Past Chair, and the Director of the DVRS shall comprise the Executive Committee.
2. The Executive Committee shall establish the agenda for the meetings of the Council, manage the Council's financial business, and ensure that the Council's membership is in compliance with state and federal mandates.
3. In the Event of an emergency, the Executive Committee is empowered to act on the Council's behalf. Such actions of the Executive Committee on behalf of the full Council shall be subject to ratification or memorialization by the Council at its next scheduled meeting.

4. Recruit and recommend new members as appropriate to keep Council membership in compliance with mandated representation. Contact non-active members.

Article XII – Committees

The chairperson shall appoint committees annually in accordance with these By-laws. In addition to the Executive Committee, there shall be four (3) Standing Committees:

1. Evaluation Committee, which shall include activities such as, but not limited to, program evaluation, consumer satisfaction, and comprehensive needs assessment.
2. Policy/ Legislative Committee, which shall include activities such as, but not limited to, policy review, education, state plan review, administrative code review, and activities relative to legislation, regulation and funding having potential to impact on DVRS and its program at federal and state government levels and in other domains as determined to apply.
3. Transition of Students and Youth to Work Committee, which shall include activities such as, but not limited to, feedback on Pre-Employment Transition Services (ETS), inform on educational issues that impact the provision of ETS, support interagency collaboration of stakeholders, and advise on Federal and State laws.

Article XIII – Amendment of By-laws

1. Recommended amendments may be submitted in writing to the By-laws Committee for their evaluation and recommendation to the full Council in accordance with Article XII (4) above.
2. To provide adequate review time, proposed amendments shall be provided to council members at least two weeks prior to the meeting at which they will be discussed and voted on.
3. Amendments to By-laws shall become effective upon the approval of at least 50 percent plus one of the voting membership of the Council.

Article XIV – Code of Conduct

1. All members and staff shall be provided with a current copy of the New Jersey State Code of Ethics and shall abide by its terms.
2. No council members shall enter into any grant or contract agreements with the Council on their own behalf.
3. No member of the Council shall vote on any matter that would provide direct financial benefit to the member or otherwise give the appearance of a conflict of interest under State law.

Article XV Removal-

1. Any Council member may be removed by the Governor.
2. If a Council member misses three (3) consecutive Council meetings, the Council may recommend to the Governor, at the discretion of the Executive Committee, the removal of the member from the Council.

Section 2:
Example of SRC Handbook

(New Jersey General SRC)

Beliefs

As members of the State Rehabilitation Council of the State of New Jersey, *We Believe* --

* Each person with a disability has value;
* People with disabilities, like all people, have diverse strengths that must be defined and identified along many dimensions;
* In a public system of vocational rehabilitation that is responsible and accountable to those it serves and to those who fund it;
* In partnerships, affiliations, and linkages;
* That optimal results in rehabilitation depend on an equal partnership between people with disabilities and the professional (service provider);
* That all people with disabilities should be given enough information to make informed choices;
* People with disabilities are ultimately responsible and accountable for the choices they make;
* That all people with disabilities should have the opportunity to maximize their potential;
* That respect to all is critical to this process;
* That it is necessary to support, further, and exemplify diversity and multiculturalism within the disability community and the community at large; and
* That the rights of people with disabilities should be advanced and protected.

Mission Statement

The State Rehabilitation Council is a partnership of people with disabilities, advocates, and other interested persons. It is committed to ensuring through policy development, implementation, and advocacy that New Jersey has a State vocational rehabilitation program that is not only comprehensive and consumer-responsive but also effective, efficient, and significantly funded. The State Rehabilitation Council is dedicated to ensuring that people with disabilities receive rehabilitation services that result in competitive, integrated employment.

The Workforce Innovation and Opportunity Act (WIOA)

WIOA was signed into law July 22, 2014, reauthorizing the Rehabilitation Act of 1973 under Title IV.

The SRC is committed to ensuring appropriate support to DVRS in carrying out the spirit, intent, and mandates of the WIOA.

Membership
Recruitment
The SRC will actively recruit new members on an ongoing basis.

- Names of possible candidates will be solicited from current members and from a broad range of organizations and people with disabilities.
- The Executive Committee will make recommendations to the Governor to bring the membership into mandated compliance as needed.

Mandated Membership

Membership shall be in accordance with the mandates of Section 105 of the Rehabilitation Act of 1973, as amended, and Section 361.16 and 361.17 of the implementing Regulations, and shall reflect a diverse range of disability groups, geographical areas, racial and ethnic groups and gender.

A majority of Council members must be people with disabilities, who are not employed by DVRS, who meet the definition of "individual with a disability"- in Section 361.5(c)(28) of the Regulations- an individual who "has a physical or mental impairment that substantially limits one or more life activities, has a record of such an impairment, or is regarded as having such an impairment".

The total number of voting members shall not exceed twenty-five (25).

See By Laws "Article VI- Membership"- page 3 for details of mandated membership categories.

Terms of Appointment

Each member of the Council must be appointed by the Governor for a term of no more than three years, and serve no more than two consecutive full terms. (Except for the Client Assistance Program representative who has no term limit.)

In order to be eligible to be reappointed following completion of two consecutive terms, a member must complete a period of two months in non-member status following the last date of the member's second term.

Meetings

Schedule

Meetings of the Council shall be held four (4) times per year. The full Council will meet during the morning session and committees will meet during the afternoon session.

An additional strategic planning meeting will be held annually.

Special meetings may be called as deemed necessary by the Executive Committee. Notification of not less than five (5) business days shall be made to all members.

A quorum (fifty percent plus one of appointed members) must be present to conduct the formal business of the Council.

Attendance

Participation in the general meetings, committee meetings, and the annual strategic planning meeting is critical to ensure a quorum and to facilitate the work of the Council. Members who miss three (3) consecutive meetings without a valid reason (medical, family, personal) will be contacted by the Executive Committee regarding their availability to continue on the Council. A letter of resignation will be requested if a member is not able to actively participate. If no letter of resignation is received, the Executive Committee may recommend to the Governor the removal of the member from the Council.

Agenda

The Executive Committee will establish the agenda for the meetings of the Council, which shall be emailed to all members no later than one week prior to the meeting date.

Sites/Accommodations

All meeting rooms and facilities will be accessible and of adequate size. Provision will be made for special modes of communication and other accommodations if requested at least one week prior to the meeting date.

Notification/Emergencies

A notification system will be put into place in the event of inclement weather or an emergency on the morning of the meetings. The Executive Committee will inform all members if a meeting is cancelled.

Each SRC member is responsible for providing the Executive Committee with current emergency contact information.

Officers

Officers: Chair, Vice-Chair, Treasurer.

Term of Office: 2 years, beginning June of even numbered years. May be elected to serve for one additional consecutive term.

Elections

The Executive Committee appoints a Nominating Committee (minimum three members not holding Council office) for officer elections at the November (odd year) meeting preceding the election year. The Nominating Committee is responsible for presenting a slate of officers to the SRC members no later than 2-weeks prior to the May election meeting (even year).

At the May meeting of the election year, the slate recommended by the nominating committee, as well as nominations made from the floor, shall be considered and an election held. A majority vote of the members present shall be required for election. (*A quorum must be present.*)

Duties

Chairperson:

- Convene and preside over the meetings of the Council.
- Appoint Standing Committees-annually.
- Appoint Ad Hoc Committees on an as needed basis.
- Perform other duties that the Council feels appropriate.
- Serve on Executive Committee for one year after term of office ends.

Vice Chairperson

- When the chairperson is not available, the vice-chairperson assumes these duties.
- Coordinate preparation of Annual Report.

Treasurer

- Prepare and submit the annual SRC budget for review and approval of the Council.
- Report on status of budget at each Council meeting.
- Maintain the financial accounts of the SRC.
- Approve requests for expenditures and reimbursements.

Mandated Functions

The SRC, on behalf of the community it represents, reviews, analyzes and advises the New Jersey State Vocational Rehabilitation Program (DVRS) regarding the performance of its responsibilities. Council goals and activities are set annually and are in response to both National and State issues, as mandated by Section 105 of the Rehabilitation Act of 1973, as amended. The focus of Council goals and activities includes but is not limited to Consumer Satisfaction, Statewide Needs Assessment, State Plan and Amendments, Policy, Extent/Scope/Effectiveness of Services, Interagency Agreements, and New Jersey's Employment programs.

- *See By Laws Article V- "Duties"- page 2- for full text of mandated duties under Section 105 of the Rehabilitation Act.*

In addition to Section 105, which mandates SRC procedures and functions, DVRS has mandates related to working with the SRC sprinkled throughout the Act:
- Jointly develop, agree to and review annually VR agency goals and priorities.
- Consult regularly re development, implementation, and revision of policies and procedures pertaining to VR services.
- Include summary of SRC input in the VR Section of the Unified or Combined State Plan.
- Jointly conduct comprehensive statewide needs assessment (CSNA) every three years.
- Review and comment on the Comprehensive System of Personnel Development (CSPD).
- Transmit copies of the following to the SRC:
    All plans, reports, and other information required to be submitted to RSA.
    All policies and information on practices and procedures provided to or used by rehabilitation personnel in carrying out the VR program.
    Due process hearing decisions (in a manner to protect individual confidentiality).

Descriptions of Major Functions

Comprehensive Statewide Needs Assessment
A comprehensive statewide needs assessment must be jointly conducted by DVRS and the Council every three years. Results of the assessment are to be included in the vocational rehabilitation portion of the Unified State Plan.

The comprehensive needs assessment must describe the rehabilitation needs of individuals with disabilities residing within the State, particularly the vocational rehabilitation services needs of—

- Individuals with the most significant disabilities, including their need for supported employment services;
- Individuals with disabilities who are minorities and individuals with disabilities who have been unserved or underserved by the vocational rehabilitation program

- Individuals with disabilities served through other components of the statewide workforce development system;
- Youth with disabilities, and students with disabilities, including their need for pre-employment transition services or other transition services; and an assessment of the needs of individuals with disabilities for transition services and pre-employment transition services, and the extent to which such services provided under this part are coordinated with transition services provided under the Individuals with Disabilities Education Act.

It also must include an assessment of the need to establish, develop, or improve community rehabilitation programs within the State.

Consumer Satisfaction Survey

The Rehabilitation Act requires the SRC to conduct, to the extent feasible, a review and analysis of the effectiveness and consumer satisfaction with vocational rehabilitation services. The services are those provided by the state agency and other private or public programs that provide VR services to people with disabilities. The survey must also include employment outcomes achieved by eligible individuals receiving services, including the availability of health and other employment benefits.

VR Section of the Unified State Plan and Attachments

The Unified State Plan describes the policies and procedures adopted by DVRS to administer the public VR program. It provides assurances that DVRS will follow all the requirements detailed in in the Rehabilitation Act. It describes how key components and processes of the Rehabilitation Act will be implemented and administered and ultimately how people with disabilities will be provided services leading to employment. The SRC is mandated to assist in the preparation of the VR portion of the Unified State Plan and amendments to the plan.

The Unified State Plan and Attachments must be submitted to RSA on or before July 1 each year.

SRC Input to the Unified State Plan

The Rehabilitation Act requires that DVRS include in the VR Section of the Unified State Plan and in any revision to the plan, a summary of input provided by the Council, including recommendations from the annual report of the Council, the review and analysis of consumer satisfaction, and other reports prepared by the Council, and the response of the designated State unit to such input and recommendations, including explanations for rejecting any input or recommendations. The Council assists in preparation of this section to ensure that SRC input and recommendations are accurate and comprehensive.

Annual Report

The Rehabilitation Act requires the SRC to prepare an Annual Report on the status of the vocational rehabilitation programs operated within the State, covering the period 10/1 to 9/30. The report must be submitted to the Governor or appropriate State entity and the Commissioner of the Rehabilitation Services Administration by December 31 and made available to the public.

The report is to be prepared and disseminated for discussion at the November Council meeting.

Public Hearings
DVRS holds public hearing meetings for the State Plan.
Public hearings are held for adoption/ re-adoption of the Administrative Code.
Public Hearings are required when entering an Order of Selection for Services.
SRC members are encouraged to actively participate when these meetings are held.

Administrative Code Review
The Administrative Code sets forth the policy that the agency follows when implementing both federal and state laws. The advice and recommendations of the SRC will be sought when developing code.

Committees

Standing Committees
Standing Committees carry out work necessary to meet the goals of the Council.
Each Council member is expected to participate on a committee.
The SRC Chairperson shall appoint committees at the Council's annual planning meeting.

There are five (5) Standing Committees:

1. Executive Committee consists of the Chairperson, Vice-Chairperson, Treasurer, Immediate Past Chair (one year), and the DVRS Director as ex- officio.
- Prepare meeting agendas.
- Manage Council's financial business.
- Coordinate Annual Unified State Plan Public Hearings.
- Contact non-active members per "Attendance" pages 4 and 5.
- Prepare as necessary a list of persons to be recommended to the Governor for appointment or re-appointment to the Council in compliance with Rehabilitation Act mandates.
- Act on Council's behalf in the event of an emergency. (Subject to ratification at next Council meeting.)

2. Evaluation Committee shall include activities such as, but not limited to:
- Program evaluation and operations of the Agency.
- Consumer Satisfaction.
- Review of SETC Consumer Report Card.

3. Policy / Legislative Committee shall include activities such as, but not limited to:
    Policy
- Review Administrative Code changes.
- Review and provide input to the VR Section of the Unified State Plan.
- Review and provide input to VR policy and revisions.
- Review and provide input to the three-year plan for the Comprehensive Statewide Needs Assessment.

<u>Legislative</u>
- Review/monitor current and pending legislation- identify issues and recommend strategies as indicated.
- Coordinate with other agencies and groups that share an interest in legislation and regulation relating to vocational rehabilitation services to people with disabilities.

4. Transition of Students and Youth to Work Committee shall include activities such as, but not limited to:

- Provide feedback to DVRS on the provision of Pre-Employment Transition Services (Pre-ETS).
- Inform DVRS and the SRC on educational issues that impact the provision of Pre-ETS.
- Support interagency collaboration among all the stakeholder agencies involved with transition issues.
- Review and advise DVRS about Federal and State laws and regulations related to Pre-ETS, education, and transition services.

5. By-laws Review Committee shall be appointed by the Chair at the Annual Strategic Planning Meeting in even numbered years to review and make recommendations to the full Council for needed revisions

Ad hoc committees, task forces, and study groups shall be created at the discretion of the Council Chairperson to evaluate Council activities and identify areas of concern for Council attention.
- At least two-thirds (2/3) of the membership of the ad hoc committees, task forces, and study groups shall be members the Council.
- Each ad hoc committee, task force, and study group shall elect a Chairperson who must be a Council member for the purposes of reporting to the Council.

Finances
Resource Plan
The Council shall prepare, in conjunction with DVRS, a plan for the provision of resources, including staff and other personnel, as may be necessary and sufficient to carry out the functions of the Council. The resource plan shall, to the maximum extent possible, rely on the use of resources in existence during the period of implementation of the plan.

The Resource Plan should be prepared and disseminated prior to the September Council meeting for approval at the September meeting.

Budget
The budget is part of the Resource Plan and shall be prepared annually by the Treasurer and approved by the Council at the September meeting.

DVRS Contracted Fiscal Agent
The fiscal agent shall perform all business office functions of the SRC including accounting and banking:

- Disburse funds as directed by the Treasurer;
- Maintain and reconcile books and records;
- Prepare periodic reports for the SRC as required by the DVRS; contract and
- Maintain separate books and records including a checking account specifically for the SRC. Allowable expenditures are only those authorized by the Treasurer within the scope of the DVRS contract budget.

Member Reimbursement

The Council may use funds appropriated under this title to reimburse members of the Council for reasonable and necessary expenses of attending Council meetings and performing Council duties.

SRC members can request (on SRC "Expense Report/ Reimbursement Request Form"- Appendix D) reimbursement for the following as appropriate and pre-approved:

- Travel: SRC-approved members will be reimbursed for pre-approved actual costs.
- Mileage* State rate.
- Tolls and Parking.
- Lodging: State rate. *
- Per Diem Meals (In or Out-of-State): State rate. *
- Personal Assistance: Pre-approved actual cost.
- Child Care: Pre-approved actual cost.
- Miscellaneous: SRC members shall submit claims for reimbursement for such items as telephone calls, copying, conversion of materials to alternative formats and other reasonable costs incurred in the performance of SRC duties within reasonable pre-approved amounts.

Actual bills or official receipts shall be submitted with the "Expense Report/Reimbursement" Request .

* http://www.gsa.gov/portal/content/104877

DVRS as Support

DVRS will provide support to assist the SRC with its responsibilities.

Liaison

The Director's Executive Assistant is the liaison to the SRC and will coordinate the support activities.

Clerical

The Director's Secretarial Assistant provides the clerical support for the SRC and coordinates the work of other clerical personnel when necessary to facilitate the work of the SRC. (She arranges for meeting sites, refreshments, special modes of communication and personal assistant services).

Technical

Program Planning and Development Specialists are available as technical support specialists. A specialist will be assigned as requested to assist SRC members with specific mandated tasks.

Accounting

The DVRS accounting specialist is available for advice and support for the SRC Treasurer or individual members regarding budgets and reimbursements.

SRC Training Resources

New Member Orientation- New members will receive a face-to-face half-day orientation as soon as is practicable after appointment.

"State Rehabilitation Council- Vocational Rehabilitation Partnership Under WIOA" available from Amazon.com.

National Coalition of State Rehabilitation Councils- (NCSRC)- (www.ncsrc.net)
Includes: History; Members; National Listserv; Links to other SRC websites; Meetings and Training dates and locations; Examples from other SRCs; WIOA resources.

Appendices

APPENDIX A: Rehabilitation Act- Section 105- State Rehabilitation Council
Signed into law July 22, 2014
Full text not included since it appears elsewhere in this document.

APPENDIX B: REGULATIONS to Implement Section 105 of the Rehabilitation Act- State Rehabilitation Council §361.16 & 361.17
Full text not included since it appears elsewhere in this document.

APPENDIX C: Executive Order No. 110(1993)- New Jersey Register- Office of the Governor- New Jersey Division of Vocational Rehabilitation Services Rehabilitation Advisory Council- Issued: October 29, 1993- Effective: October 29, 1993- Expiration: Indefinite
Full text not applicable to other states and therefore not included here.

APPENDIX D:
NEW JERSEY STATE REHABILITATION COUNCIL
EXPENSE REPORT/REIMBURSEMENT REQUEST
Full text not included since requirements vary by state.

Section 3:
Example of SRC Operating Procedures

(Oklahoma)

I. Membership
A. Recruitment
1. The proposed applicant will receive application forms within 10 days of their acceptance to be on ORC
2. Applicant will complete and submit all forms to the Program Manager (PM) within 30 days of receipt of application
3. PM responsibilities
   a) Submit completed applications to Governor's Appointment Director within 5 days
   b) Maintain pool of prospective candidates in appropriate membership composition categories
   c) Attend events that may lend opportunities for recruiting new members
   d) Annual communication with Governor's Appointment Director to ensure membership composition.

B. Orientation
1. PM is responsible for conducting orientation to new member prior to the attendance of first quarterly meeting, but within 30 days of appointment, whichever comes first
2. Assist new member in making a committee selection at orientation

C. Member Roles and Responsibilities
1. Attend quarterly meetings and annual meeting regularly
2. Active committee participation through meeting attendance, in-person or conference call, and research if needed
3. Notification to PM regarding any absence(s)

D. Replacement
1. Term limits as determined in By-Laws
2. Resignation
   a) EC may request voluntary resignation of any member who fails to carry out their council responsibilities (i.e., 3 unexcused absences at quarterly or committee meetings, disruptive behavior at meetings, personal agenda that is not in keeping with the ORC mission, etc.)
3. PM responsibilities
   a) 3 months prior to member term limit – PM will provide to EC, a list of any first or second term limited members
   b) PM and EC will review to ensure timely replacement

c) PM will contact the members to communicate either continuance or term limit with last meeting responsibility

d) PM will contact Governor's Appointment Director to provide either continuance or new appointment information

e) PM will contact any potential new member(s) to discuss membership interest within 5 days of EC recommendation

II.   Responsibilities of ORC Chair
A. Attendance
1.   All meetings with Director and Division Administrators
2.   All EC and Quarterly meetings
3.   Committee meetings when possible
4.   At least one of each set of the Public Hearings (State Plan and Policy)
5.   At least one CSAVR meeting annually
6.   The Disability Awareness Day at the Capitol annually
7.   The in-state legislative visits, whenever possible

B.   10 business days prior to quarterly meeting, ORC Chair will provide PM with written report summarizing quarterly activities or recommendations to vote on any action items.

III. Committees Chairs
A. Executive Committee
1. Within 2 weeks prior to annual Strategic Planning Committee Meeting, EC will review the purpose/function of each committee to ensure that it continues to meet the needs of the ORC

2. Implement Nomination Committee process

3. Approval of nominees

4. If necessary recommend to the Governor's office removal of any current member(s)

5. Ensure a committee is assigned to meet the requirements of Section 105 of the Rehab Act with regard to the following annual activities

a) Public Hearings

b) State Plan

c) Comprehensive Needs Assessment

d) Customer Satisfaction

e) Annual Report

    i.   Review draft of annual report within 7 business days of receipt

6. Attendance

a) Meetings with Director and Division Administrators, when possible

b) At a minimum 3 of the Quarterly meetings and EC meetings

c) At the yearly Strategic Planning meeting

d) Committee Chair will appointment committee member to report at quarterly meeting in the event of their absence

7. PM responsibilities

a) 10 days prior to ORC Executive meeting with Division Administrators and Director, PM will send request for agenda items to be included on the shared agenda; Have minutes of Division Administrators and Director meetings completed and sent to attendees

B. Policy & Legislative Committee

1. Facilitate a minimum of 4 committee meetings annually
2. Attendance
   a) At a minimum of 3 of the Quarterly meetings and EC meetings
   b) Meetings with Director and Division Administrators, when possible
   c) To at least one of the Public Hearings on Policy, annually
   d) To the spring CSAVR meeting annually
   e) The Disability Awareness Day at the Capitol annually
   f) The in-state legislative visits, when possible
3. Active participation on the DRS Policy Re-engineering Committee
4. 10 business days prior to quarterly meeting, Chair will provide PM with written report summarizing quarterly activities or recommendations to vote on any action items

C. Transition Committee
1. Facilitate a minimum of 4 committee meetings annually
2. Attendance
   a) At a minimum of 3 of the Quarterly meetings and EC meetings
   b) Meetings with Director and Division Administrators, when possible
   c) The Disability Awareness Day at the Capitol annually
3. Active participation on the Oklahoma Transition Council
4. Must participate at the annual Oklahoma Transition Institute
5. 10 business days prior to quarterly meeting, Chair will provide PM with written report summarizing quarterly activities or recommendations to vote on any action items

D. Program and Planning Committee
1. Facilitate a minimum of 4 committee meetings annually
2. Attendance
   a) At a minimum of 3 of the Quarterly meetings and EC meetings
   b) Meetings with Director and Division Administrators, when possible
   c) At least one of the Public Hearings on State Plan, annually
   d) The Disability Awareness Day at the Capitol annually, when possible
3. Active participation on the DRS State Plan meetings
4. Active participation on the DRS Comprehensive Needs Assessment development initiative
5. Analyze the trends of the Customer Satisfaction Survey
6. 10 business days prior to quarterly meeting, Chair will provide PM with written report summarizing quarterly activities or recommendations to vote on any action items

E. Employment Committee
Facilitate a minimum of 4 committee meetings annually
2. Attendance
   a) At a minimum of 3 of the Quarterly meetings and EC meetings
   b) Meetings with Director and Division Administrators, when possible
   c) The Disability Awareness Day at the Capitol annually
3. Active participation with the Business Services Team at DRS

5. 10 business days prior to quarterly meeting, Chair will provide PM with written report summarizing quarterly activities or recommendations to vote on any action items

IV. Committee

A. Committees will carry out their objectives as determined through the ORC Annual Strategic Plan

B. Each committee will submit a final report at the last quarterly meeting of the fiscal year, with regard to the committee's accomplishments, challenges and recommendations for inclusion in the annual report

C. Ad-Hock committees will comply with Standard Operating Procedures

D. PM Responsibilities
1. Within 30 days of each quarterly meeting, seek input from Committee members to determine next committee meeting date and assist with scheduling committee meeting
2. Provide each committee member, when possible, with a 2 week advance meeting notification
3. Track activities for each committee – assign time lines when needed
4. Provide written notes of all meetings and submit to committee chairs within 5 business days

V. Quarterly/Annual Meetings

A. Preparation - PM responsibilities
1. 10 days prior to quarterly meeting send reminder to Field Coordinators with the reporting template with a return deadline for template to be included in meeting packet
2. Assist with preparation of any agenda or other documentation to ensure individual accommodations
3. 30 days prior to quarterly meeting, request quarterly reports from all committee chairs with a due date no later than 10 business days prior to meeting but never to be later than 7 business days prior to meeting
4. 30 days prior to quarterly meeting, request all needed materials, documentation, reports from Division Administrators and other appropriate agency personnel with a due date no later than 10 business days prior to meeting but never to be later than 7 days prior to meeting
5. Provide quarterly meeting notification to entire membership 5 business days prior to meeting – meeting notification should include electronic packet which contains agenda, draft minutes, committee reports and any other necessary documentation to conduct business
6. Provide for interpreter/food/room arrangement/materials accommodation needs and meet Open Meeting Act requirement

B. Post Meeting - PM Responsibilities
1. Within one week of quarterly meeting, PM will follow up on any action items or issues that were discussed during the meeting
2. Within 30 days of quarterly meeting, PM will provide Chair with draft of quarterly meeting minutes
3. Repeat preparation process

VI. Annual Report

A. PM Responsibilities

1. Complete draft of annual report 30 days after end of fiscal year and share with EC
2. Once approved by the full ORC, prepare for print
3. Submit final annual report to RSA and all stakeholders as outlined in Section 105 of the Rehab Act by December 31st of each year
4. Post on the ORC web site

VII. Accommodations

    A. ORC will act consistent with the Americans with Disabilities Act (ADA), Section 504 and 508 of the Rehabilitation Act, and Oklahoma 508 law

1. Facilities barrier free
2. Provide for reasonable accommodations to individuals with disabilities who request them
   a) unless the ORC can demonstrate that making the modifications would fundamentally alter the nature of the service, program, or activity
3. Take appropriate steps to ensure that communications with applicants, participants, and members of the public with disabilities are as effective as communications with others
4. Provide appropriate auxiliary aids, services, including personal assistant services, driver services, interpreter services, reader services, etc. during their term of membership
5. Primary consideration to the requests of the individual with disabilities
6. The individual requesting the accommodation must specify the type of accommodation to the ORC Program Manager in a reasonable time frame to allow for the accommodation to be provided when requested
7. Assistive Technology purchased for members remains the property of the ORC

Section 4:
Example of SRC Input to the Unified State Plan

(West Virginia SRC)

The West Virginia Division of Rehabilitation Services (DRS) received input from the West Virginia State Rehabilitation Council (SRC) members and chairman regarding the Unified State Plan to be submitted by the Workforce Innovation and Opportunity Act partners in 2018. The following is the summary submitted to the agency by the Council with observations, recommendations and the agency responses:

The West Virginia State Rehabilitation Council (WV SRC) is extremely proud to be a vital, supportive partner of the West Virginia Division of Rehabilitation Services (WV DRS). For several years, the agency has continued to receive national recognition for the unique programs and diverse services helping to ensure that people in West Virginia with disabilities reach and maintain their individual employment goals.

Our Council is comprised of individuals from throughout West Virginia who represent many differing backgrounds that includes business, labor & industry, Client Assistant Program (CAP), Community Rehabilitation Programs (CRPs), other services providers, Vocational Rehabilitation counselors, Workforce Investment Board, West Virginia Department of Education, consumers and consumer advocates. This unwavering partnership demonstrated the core of our mission and vision by allowing the Council insight of consumer needs.

WV DRS provides beneficial updates when making presentations to our membership during Council meetings or as needed. We greatly appreciate the former WV DRS liaison to our Council, Michael Meadows and the newly appointed liaison Rich Ward, who are both considered a valuable asset and informed resource by our members. Sharing agency data regarding programs, services, fiscal status or other pertinent issues is invaluable. Policy development and implementation is a major role of the Council and under the guidance of Assistant Director of Field Services Susan Weinberger, the Council has a collective interest in assuring the agency achieves the utmost level of quality assurance to serve West Virginians.

West Virginia is one of the few states to have achieved this feat. Senior Manager of State Plan and Program Evaluation Pisnu Bua-Iam had assured that all members have a clear understanding of what this means to the agency and allows time for members to ask questions during his regular presentations. With the continuing changes in the law, Mr. Bua-Iam and his staff continues to educate our Council members that WV DRS has exceeded other states in this realm. The WV SRC understands the agency's obligation in achieving the highest performance benchmarks that were set by the Rehabilitation Services Administration (RSA).

The WV SRC is pleased to present the ongoing comments for modification of the Unified State Plan for Program Year (PY) 2018 to the WV DRS:

Observation 1

The agency strives to educate the general public regarding the WV DRS office locations to ensure knowledge and the continuum of agency services and programs. The agency utilizes newspaper articles, statewide magazine advertisements, community events, social media and public broadcasting as a means to assure awareness of the available services within WV DRS in all areas of the state.

Recommendation: The WV SRC recommends this practice be continued with a continuing emphasis directed into underserved areas of the State.

DRS Response to Observation/Recommendation 1
DRS agrees with the recommendation to continue efforts to inform the general public about the availability of DRS services. In recent years, the agency has focused on reaching out to stakeholders of vocational rehabilitation (VR) services, including potentially underserved/unserved areas of the state. DRS utilizes the latest technology for this purpose, including a web map that includes turn—by—turn directions to each office to help potential consumers more easily find DRS field offices. Additional activities include the sponsoring of community events and statewide radio advertisements. In Program Years (PYs) 2018-2019, DRS plans to continue to identify efficient and cost-effective ways to reach out to consumers with disabilities, including potentially underserved/unserved populations using various methods such as cross-promotion among the Workforce Innovation and Opportunity Act (WIOA) core partners (WorkForce WV, WV Adult Education, and DRS) within the WV workforce development system. Additionally, with the ongoing implementation of the WIOA, an additional focus for DRS is to reach out to students with disabilities, including their parents and service providers in the community. These outreach activities are discussed below in later responses.

Observation 2
A priority for WV DRS is reaching students during their secondary education (9th — 12th grades) for it is imperative to start early in identifying career paths. Establishing an Individual Plan for Employment (IPE) early to outline a vocational goal area and necessary services needed to support this goal is important for a student's success when transitioning from High School to the next phase of life whether this being continuing education or employment. The agency has VR counselors assigned to all secondary schools in West Virginia with offices physically located in high schools in West Virginia — Brooke, Cabell Midland, Huntington, John Marshall, Parkersburg South, Preston County, Wheeling Park and Woodrow Wilson High Schools.

Uncertainties continue that once students are preparing to leave the secondary school system and move forward into higher education that students, parents and their advisors/counselors may not be fully aware of services available through DRS. Placing Pathways banners at all West Virginia high schools will also increase awareness of available transition resources for students.

Recommendation: The WV SRC recommends working with high schools and/or vocational schools to establish VR offices to be physically located on the campus of those selected schools. This would provide more access to VR counselors and assistance to those students and their families in an effort to gain applicants for services at an earlier age as funding allows.

DRS Response to Observation/Recommendation 2
DRS agrees that it is important for students with disabilities to begin the vocational rehabilitation process as early as appropriate. DRS is open to the recommendation and has requested that counselors identify any possible opportunities for embedded VR offices within high schools. If

opportunities arise, DRS will move forward to establish offices, where appropriate and agreed upon by both parties.

In support of this aim, DRS has a vocational rehabilitation counselor assigned to each high school in the state. During PYs 2016-2017, DRS placed large banners in high schools in all 55 WV counties and in almost every high school in the state. These banners provide information on DRS' PathwaysWV.org website for students with disabilities. The website also provides access to additional information on ways to access services from DRS.

Observation 3
With the demographics and cultural backgrounds of West Virginia, effective communication must be innovative. Finding the most efficient avenue to educate students and their families regarding available WV DRS services and programs is a continuing challenge. Effective, good communication is a key factor.

Recommendation: The WV SRC recommends that WV DRS: continue to keep students and their families abreast about services and programs offered by the agency through social media; and, increase access to VR staff assigned to their respective schools by making school presentations, using VR displays, exhibiting posters in prominent locations and having an increased presence at Individual Education Plans (IEPs) and other transition planning meetings.

DRS Response to Observation/Recommendation 3
DRS agrees that effective, good communication is a key factor in making sure that students with disabilities and their families are aware of DRS services and programs that are available for eligible individuals as they begin preparing for post—secondary school goals. DRS engages in a variety of outreach activities to ensure widespread information dissemination that is beneficial for students with disabilities preparing to leave the school setting. These activities include sponsoring community events, attending job fairs, passing out brochures, student—focused radio advertisements, and speaking to classrooms.

In PYs 2016-2017, DRS collaborated with the WV Department of Education to develop and provide students and parents with disability-related and transition resource guides. These guides were initially distributed by the WV Department of Education to all students in special education, with future distributions for all 6th and 9th graders in special education each year. These guides serve as a marketing/recruiting tool for DRS in addition to providing valuable resource information to students and parents. DRS has also collaborated with the Mid—Ohio Valley Workforce Board to assist in developing and disseminating an employment guide to each high school guidance counselor and DRS counselor working with high school students in the region's nine counties.

Additionally, the agency has a counselor assigned to each high school in West Virginia as well as liaisons assigned to institutions of higher education around the state. This on—site presence assists the agency in developing and maintaining working relationships, on a personal level, with students and school staff. Counselors provide outreach materials, including a specialized brochure for transition students. The brochure highlights the DRS Transition program, including eligibility requirements and available services. The brochure has the agency's website address where additional information about the DRS Transition program is available. DRS will continue to explore new, effective methods of information dissemination to secondary schools and institutions of higher education. Furthermore, DRS will continue to consult with state and local education officials regarding the use of newsletters and registration packets to inform students and their families about DRS services.

Observation 4
The partnership between WV DRS and the Department of Education is imperative for the successful transition of students into the workforce. To reinforce this partnership, the need for preserving open communication is a vital component to assure students are referred to vocational rehabilitation at a younger age and have an informed understanding of community based services offered by WV DRS.

Recommendation: The WV SRC recommends this component be continued to strengthen knowledge of policies, referral processes as well as emerging trends and practices on an annual basis.

DRS Response to Observation/Recommendation 4
DRS agrees with the Council's recommendation to continue to strengthen the link between the agency and the public school system, as this link is considered vital to the continued referral of students with disabilities. DRS continues to maintain a strong connection and working relationship with the West Virginia Department of Education, as well as the county—level Boards of Education. The agency has updated its Memorandums of Understanding with the WV Department of Education and all 55 County Boards of Education to reflect changes concerning Section 511 and pre-employment transition services (pre-ETS). With the implementation of WIOA, DRS has increased collaborative efforts with school staff at the state and local level, particularly regarding the provision of pre—employment transition services to high school students with disabilities beginning in the tenth grade.

Since 2015, DRS has partnered with the WV Department of Education for Graduation 20/20, aimed at increasing the high school graduation rates of students with disabilities. In 2016, DRS Counselors, LEA staff, and Regional Educational Service Agency staff participated in multiple cross-training events to learn about pre-ETS, and to develop ideas for collaborative provision. Existing projects and programs in the state were highlighted, some of which were later duplicated in other areas. DRS Counselors joined local Graduation 20/20 teams across the state; Pre-ETS activities were coordinated and used as a strategy to not only promote graduation, but also encourage competitive, integrated employment for all students with disabilities.

In consultation with DRS, the WV Office of Special Education amended its policies to demonstrate compliance with WIOA Section 511, and include pre-ETS on the Individualized Education Plan (IEP). Additionally, the WV Department of Education plans to reduce the age at which Transition must be addressed on the IEP from 16 to 14 by the year 2019. Therefore, education and VR partners demonstrate alignment of not only WIOA and IDEA regulations, but also a shared vision of all students with disabilities offered the same transition service opportunities. After the implementation of the new policies, DRS and WV Department of Education staff conducted cross-trainings across the state. Those in attendance were County Special Education Directors, teachers, principals, IEP Specialists, and case managers. Staff were instructed on how to involve DRS Counselors in the coordination and provision of Pre-ETS for students with disabilities through the Transition Services Planner. Additionally, staff were instructed on how and when to use and distribute other transition materials for the tracking of and referral to pre-ETS and other transition services.

Observation 5

Transportation issues persist as a state and national concern. The lack of personal and public transportation in many areas of our state continues to be a repeated challenge. WV DRS offers varying opportunities for instruction in learning to drive when barriers are present. All West Virginia high schools currently offer their students driver's education classes.

Recommendation: Considering the long-term goal for all students is to be employed, the Council suggests that VR counselors stress that Individual Plans for Employment (IPEs) include driver's education assessments for students with disabilities who may require accommodations in order to drive. This may require occupational and/or developmental visual evaluations. Any driver education instructor in the state should be supplied with the information available outlining the agency's driving program that offers technical and adaptive support or training.

DRS Response to Observation/Recommendation 5

DRS agrees that driving and transportation in general are often a barrier to employment for West Virginians with disabilities of all ages. DRS continues to seek solutions to transportation issues and maintains this as an agency goal and priority. DRS will continue to make sure that consumers are aware of these options and continue to identify targeted solutions to the varied transportation issues for West Virginians with disabilities, focusing specifically on individualized transportation solutions. During the initial phase of the vocational rehabilitation process, DRS counselors discuss transportation—related issues with consumers. Counselors work with consumers to address and resolve any identified disability—related employment barriers; services to circumvent barriers are included in Individualized Plans for Employment and may include transportation services.

Observation 6

In looking toward the future, the agency expects an influx of youth who have drug and/or alcohol related issues and will need services. The agency is not only concerned about the youth having substance related disorders of their own, but also the long term effects of prenatal opiate exposure.

This will be an area that will require VR staff to have more diverse training in these specialized programs and skill sets.

Recommendation: The WV SRC recommends that the Agency continues to provide staff with the training and technical assistance needed to expand their knowledge of drug addiction related diseases.

DRS Response to Observation/Recommendation 6

DRS agrees with the issues raised by the SRC regarding the potential increase in the number of consumers having drug and/or alcohol related issues. In addition to the implementation of a Behavioral Health and Correction Specialist at the state level, DRS has been proactive in this area in recent years by providing training to counselors. Training has occurred at the State Training Conference in the past and will continue to take place at future conferences and/or training events, as appropriate. This training will assist counselors in enhancing their service provision to individuals with addiction by providing an overview of the disease of addiction and an examination of historic, current, and future treatment modalities.

Observation 7
With the national trend focusing on working more closely with individuals who are within the corrections system who have disabilities, WV DRS has implemented a position for a Behavioral Health and Corrections Specialist. The focus will be on individuals with mental illness or other cognitive disabilities. Even though the agency works with the correctional system, providing more in depth, early intervention services to this underserved group of individuals will be of benefit.

Recommendation: The WVSRC recommends that the Agency continue to expand relationships with the Behavioral Health and Corrections communities in order to expand opportunities for these individuals with disabilities being served by these Agencies.

DRS Response to Observation/Recommendation 7
DRS agrees with the SRC about the importance of working with organizations and individuals with behavioral health issues and previous incarcerations, including individuals in juvenile detention programs. As mentioned, the agency has implemented a Behavioral Health and Corrections Specialist to focus on outreach and comprehensive service provision to these individuals. The specialist will continue to develop and maintain working relationships with related national and state organizations, assist in the training of counselors in these specialized areas, and ensure that the agency is providing quality and timely services to these individuals. In PYs 2016-2017, DRS has worked with many agencies and organizations relating to behavioral health and corrections including the WV Division of Corrections, the Office of Institutional Education Programs, the WV Bureau for Medical Services, the WV Bureau for Behavioral Health and Health Facilities, the Governor's Summit on Alcohol and Drug Use in Higher Education, the WV Behavioral Health Planning Council, and the WV Division of Juvenile Services.

Observation 8
In the past when funding allowed, WV DRS has conducted VR State Conferences every two years. Speakers from a myriad of areas have been brought to this conference to expand knowledge, update staff on new regulations, changes in the law and bring new creative ideas for program and service delivery. These conferences also provided the opportunity for the VR staff from throughout the state to spend several days sharing experiences, understanding agency issues, Client Assistance Program (CAP) training, talking with guest speakers while networking with administrative staff and their peers.

Recommendation: Promoting team building and giving the opportunity for an educational experience to enhance job performances is vital to the continuing success of the agency and enriching staff. The Council encourages the agency to continue this means of edification and reinforcement for staff, as funding permits. Agency Quality Assurance professionals should keep staff abreast of emerging practices, policy changes and trends in the respective districts.

DRS Response to Observation/Recommendation 8

DRS agrees that the Annual State Training Conference is extremely valuable for agency staff members. The conference provides expert speakers, training sessions, and networking opportunities for field staff from across the state. Additionally, it is an enriching experience for staff members to meet others from across the state. The conference promotes cohesiveness among VR staff, as well as promoting team building, in order to serve consumers with disabilities statewide. Due to budget constraints, the Annual State Training Conference will only be held when funding is available. However, the agency will continue to provide training sessions and networking opportunities to staff members through the Quality Assurance Unit and District meetings, as appropriate.

We are grateful that Mrs. Waldron and her staff have open communication with the WV SRC and the continuous support received from the agency staff. When meeting with other SRCs and VR agencies nationally, we are reminded that our working relationship is rare. Both the WV SRC and WV DRS serve as a pacesetter and mentor to other states who are eager to replicate the relationship, our accomplishments and successful structure. This is unquestionably humbling. The Council will continue to preserve this collaboration and will embrace the opportunity to serve as a dependable partner and trusted confidant of the WV DRS.

The Council congratulates the WV DRS leadership and staff for your achievements, recognition and purpose to provide essential services and programs while meeting the benchmarks set by RSA. Should you have any questions regarding these comments, please feel free to contact the WV SRC office at (304) 356-2089.

Section 5:
Example of SRC Guidebook for RSA Monitoring Visit (West Virginia)

The West Virginia State Rehabilitation Council created a guide with an index and dividers for easy access to the Council's data. This was given to the monitoring team as the SRC Executive Committee entered the meeting room. The guidebook included:

1. Letter by executive director and chair welcoming and thanking RSA for meeting with council representatives
2. Provided pictures of executive committee members who were meeting with the RSA team so they would recognize the member when talking.
3. Roster with appointment terms
4. SRC Mission & Vision
5. Council Purpose
6. SRC meeting schedule for three (3) years
7. Accomplishments, goals, objectives
8. Council Bylaws
9. SRC Policies
10. Council committees & structure
11. Council minutes for the prior year
12. Financial reports for the past year (including last compilation report)
13. Executive Director reports for the previous year
14. Annual agreement with DRS
15. Consumer satisfaction survey data: copy of survey, cover letter sent with survey, last annual consumer satisfaction survey summary report
16. SRC annual report for the previous three (3) years
17. Incorporation papers
18. NCSRC proclamation & history
19. Letter to DRS with Unified State Plan recommendations & copy of DRS response
20. DRS corrective action responses of State Plans for the previous three (3) years

Other suggestions or additions:

Pictures of displays when participating at events
Pictures of council members participating in activities

Section 6:
Example Worksheet: Membership Composition Mandates

Annual SRC Rollover Date: _____

Mandated Positions (As cited in Section 105 of the Rehabilitation Act of 1973, as amended)	Name & Residence	Voting Member	Ex Officio	Disability Y/N	Term Started	Term End
At least one representative of the Statewide Independent Living Council established under Section 705, whose representative may be the chairperson or other designee of the council						
At least one representative of a parent training and information center established pursuant to Section 682(a) of the Individuals with Disabilities Education Act						
At least one representative of the Client Assistance Program established under Section 112						
At least one qualified vocational rehabilitation counselor, with knowledge of and experience with vocational rehabilitation programs, who shall serve as an ex officio, nonvoting member of the council if the counselor is an employee of the designated state agency						
At least one representative of community rehabilitation program service providers						
Four representatives of business, industry, and labor (to include at least one representative of the State Workforce Investment board)						
Representatives of disability advocacy groups representing a cross-section of (1) individuals with physical, cognitive, sensory, and mental disabilities and (2) individuals' representatives of individuals with disabilities who have difficulty in representing themselves or are unable due to their						

Mandated Positions (As cited in Section 105 of the Rehabilitation Act of 1973, as amended)	Name & Residence	Voting Member	Ex Officio	Disability Y/N	Term Started	Term End
disabilities to represent themselves						
Current or former applicants for, or recipients of, vocational rehabilitation services						
In a state in which one or more projects are carried out under Section 121, at least one representative of the directors of the projects						
At least one representative of the state educational agency responsible for the public education of students with disabilities who are eligible to receive services under this title and Part B of the Individuals with Disabilities Education Act						
Director of designated state unit						
TOTAL: